THE WAY MAKERS

AMBASSADORS FOR CHRIST
PREPARING THE WAY OF THE LORD

ANGELA M. GRACEY, PHR

Copyright © 2014 by Angela M. Gracey, PHR

The Way Makers
Ambassadors for Christ, Preparing the Way of the Lord
by Angela M. Gracey, PHR

Printed in the United States of America

ISBN 9781498421720

All rights reserved solely by the author. The author guarantees all contents are original and do not infringe upon the legal rights of any other person or work. No part of this book may be reproduced in any form without the permission of the author. The views expressed in this book are not necessarily those of the publisher.

Scripture quotations taken from the New International Version (NIV). Copyright © 1973, 1978, 1984, 2011 by Biblica, Inc.™. Used by permission. All rights reserved.

www.xulonpress.com

Dear Mazelle,

My prayer that this book will bless you and give a glimpse into your role as an Ambassador of Christ — a messenger of God.

Co-laboring with you,
Nun Angela Gracey

Dedicated To:

My amazing husband, **Anthony E. Gracey**, whose love, support and patience made it easy for me to obey God! Thank you, honey, for standing by me, providing for me and never giving up on me. Through all of the ups and downs, you never complained. You are my very own, special *"way maker"*! You are the one whom my soul loves!

I can't say enough about my special and dear friend, **Sharon Moore**, who was with me from the beginning of this journey. Sharon, you are a constant and faithful friend, sister and prayer partner. Thank you for being my confident, sounding board, advisor...I have such a treasure in you! What can I say? We have history and we have stories! Lots of stories! I love sharing and making them with you! We also share a love for God and writing. I love you very much.

I smile as I acknowledge a very special person: **Prophetess Maria Nock**. Yvonne and I share the exact same birthday, middle name and our spouses are both named "Anthony"! God, in His divine providence, brought us together. She is affectionately called "My Elizabeth" because the very first time I shared my vision for this project with her she exploded in her spiritual language and shouted "Heyyyyyyy! Glory to God! Hallelujah!!" That's what happens every time! Her baby leaps in her womb! Maria, you have been a spiritual midwife to me. Your love, encouragement, and support bless me beyond measure. Thank you for being my champion in the spirit!

I would also like to thank **Rose Gayle** who always believed in me and prayed me through. Your love and support made my life richer and wiser and sweeter.

To the late **Granny Sydney**, who prayed me through: "Thank you for praying for me."

To my congregation at **Randolph Village:** Thank you for allowing me the honor and privilege of serving you for six years. You validate my ministry, and you always have a special place in my heart.

Finally, I say "thank you" to my mother, **Marian Pretlow,** who raised me to be a leader, not a follower.

"The Way Makers"
Ambassadors for Christ,
Preparing *the Way* of the Lord
By Angela M. Gracey, PHR

Table of Contents

PART ONE
Preparing ***The Way*** of The Lord
IN THE LIFE OF A BELIEVER

Foreword xiii
INTRODUCTION xix
CHAPTER 1   The Making of a Way Maker 27
CHAPTER 2   The Call of the Way Maker 107
CHAPTER 3   The Characteristics of a Way Maker 125
CHAPTER 4   The Role of a Way Maker 132
CHAPTER 5   The Message of a Way Maker .. 144
CHAPTER 6   The Mission of a Way Maker 151
CHAPTER 7   The Prayer of a Way Maker 165
CHAPTER 8   The Commissioning of a Way Maker 183

PART TWO
Preparing The Way Of The Lord
IN THE HOUSE OF THE LORD

INTRODUCTION 189
CHAPTER 9   The Changing of the Guard 193
CHAPTER 10 A Way Maker in Your Household 203
CHAPTER 11 Way Makers in the House of God 210
CHAPTER 12 The Anointing of Order 232
CHAPTER 13 Turning Passion Into Purpose! 248

Acknowledgements

———⸻♦⸻———

Bishop C. Milton Grannum, Ed.D., Pastor of New Covenant Church of Philadelphia – My spiritual "dad" who raised me as a Christian – You were always more than just a Pastor to me. You were my boss, counselor and mentor. You married me to a wonderful man, whom I'm proud to say that our union is 18 years strong! Your counsel brought reconciliation between me and my father, and because of that, my lifelong dream to have my own father walk me down the aisle came true! I would not be the woman I am today were it not for your ministry. It was under your leadership that I served in almost every area of Church service! Under your care and guidance, I grew in wisdom, stature and in favor with God and man. Thank you so very much, from the bottom of my heart.

Bishop Gilbert Coleman, Pastor of Freedom Christian Bible Fellowship – Thank you for allowing God to use you so powerfully to speak into my life. You have prophesied destiny for my husband and I from the first time we set foot in your Church! You gave us a place of safety to be healed and restored. My heart is especially warmed and grateful for the care I received when I went through the most frightening, life-threatening, physical illness in my entire life. When I returned to Church for the first time following that ordeal, as always, God used you to speak to me so profoundly! We miss you very much (although our leaving was prophesied by you!). Still, we look forward to seeing you on our next visit. May the blessings, favor and peace of God rest upon your life, your family and ministry.

Charles Schmitt, Pastor, Immanuel's Church – I would be remiss to have completed this work without giving honor to the leadership that allowed me to "walk out" this message. It was here where God opened so many doors for ministry: teaching, my first international missions trip, professional and ministry leadership training, inner healing and restoration, public ministry, and finally, ordination as a Minister of the Gospel. I've grown so much as a professional and as a minister under your leadership. You have

Acknowledgements

supported me and my family in amazingly significant ways, and for that I will always be grateful. Thank you and may God bless you and your family.

Foreword

The Commissioning of a Way Maker

About five years into my walk with the Lord, I responded to His specific calling on my life, through His Spirit-breathed word in Jeremiah Chapter 1. I was then led into the wilderness, by the Holy Spirit, which signaled the beginning of my season of preparation. From then until now, God has walked with me through diverse trials and tribulations that taught me how to know, lean on, and trust Him as well as obey His Word. I experienced the "dark night of the soul": confusion, God's absence (or so it seemed) and isolation. Betrayal, dying to myself, the test of significance, the stripping of selfish ambition, and overcoming my *identity crisis* were all part of the preparation process. Even so, during that season of preparation (and testing), I received God's abundant grace, physical and inner healing, restoration, guidance, and divine provision. Although I continue to allow God to prepare

The Way Makers

me for all His future plans, for the purposes of this book, let me take you back to the beginning: *the conception.*

In 2001, my husband, Anthony, and I entered a new worship relationship with Freedom Christian Bible Fellowship, in Philadelphia, Pennsylvania, under the leadership of Bishop Gilbert Coleman. Both of us had just completed their New Members' Class; the night of our graduation, unbeknownst to me, my life would change in a most profound way.

It was customary for Bishop Coleman to prophesy over each New Members' Class, as the Holy Spirit led. I had never experienced this before; in fact, being under prophetic leadership was new to my husband and myself. For the past thirteen years, I had been raised in the Kingdom by a strong teaching ministry; so, Freedom Christian Bible Fellowship was different. Prior to the graduation, I was selected to be our Class' speaker for the evening. I was very nervous as I tried to convey what the Lord put on my heart about our membership journey. Then, it was time for Bishop Coleman to address our Class; I could feel my heart beating faster as the excitement grew in anticipation of what God would say to us through him.

He declared, "You shall be called The Way Makers!" I can only paraphrase for you the essence of what he said because it was one of those surreal moments in my life, where I

Foreword

knew–beyond a shadow of a doubt–that God was speaking directly to **me**! He went on to say that God was calling our class to be an end-time army **to prepare the way** for the second coming of our Lord Jesus Christ. He said that there would be trials and tests because of the calling God had for our class. Then Bishop Coleman looked directly at me and, laying hands on me, he declared, "You are a Way Maker, and God is going to use you to raise up "Way Makers" all over the world!" It was as if God spoke directly to me! It was a divine encounter; one I would never forget, and one that would shape my destiny. That day a seed was planted and ***I became pregnant with vision***.

From that moment on, my life changed. I did not know how it was going to happen or when, but God had invited me to join Him in what He was doing. It would take more years of preparation; yet, the first trimester was already quite spectacular!

Three years later, in 2004, my husband and I relocated to Silver Spring, Maryland. We began attending Immanuel's Church (Immanuel's) because I recognized the wife of the senior pastor from a previous women's retreat. Her ministry was quite memorable and when I recognized her, I felt it was a leading from the Lord to worship at Immanuel's. The next year, in 2005, we joined Immanuel's and the following year, I found myself, again, serving in full-time ministry on their staff. I had only been employed a couple of months when God stepped in. Immanuel's would be hosting a special women's conference–after a two-year hiatus; so, all the members were particularly excited. The theme of the conference was: "Preparing The Way of the Lord." I know–can you believe it?

In preparation for the conference, the Women's Ministry planned a kick-off event–a women's breakfast–and guess who was asked to be the main speaker? You guessed it: me! By now, I saw the hand of God and I knew that was another Divine appointment! My excitement turned to panic. I cried out to God, "What in the world am I going to share with these women?" I felt added pressure since this was the first time I had been asked to speak at Immanuel's. I was aware of the significance of this moment in light of the vision God had given me; I desperately wanted to honor Him and be obedient to His leading. So, what was I going to share? I heard a still, small voice say, "You are going to tell them about The Way Makers." June 17, 2006, was the date of the women's breakfast and the start of the second trimester. These were the days of small beginnings.

In 2007, I joined the Adjunct Faculty of Logos Christian College's Bible Institute and "The Way Makers" course was born. The course was a ministry leadership development study, designed to equip the Body of Christ to prepare The Way of the Lord by

Foreword

declaring the message of reconciliation (2 Cor. 5:11–6:2); illustrated through the life John the Baptist. Participants were encouraged to allow God to first bring reconciliation and wholeness into their own lives, and then allow God to equip them as able ministers, known as *Ambassadors for Christ*!

However, God was calling me to come up higher. It was time to for me to step out in faith and trust Him to do what I could not do on my own. The scriptures state, in Hebrews 11:6, "...without faith it is impossible to please God, because anyone who comes to him must believe that he exists and that he rewards those who earnestly seek him" Heb. 11:6. I needed to walk at a greater level of faith if I was going to fulfill my God-given vision. In 2008, I experienced my biggest growth spurt in faith: I was invited to do a train-the-trainers workshop in the country of South Sudan! It was my first Missions Trip! During this adventure, I learned to trust God to supply all of my needs and the needs of those He called me to serve in a war-torn country. It was an awesome assignment from God and I returned to the United States a changed servant, who had experienced yet another divine encounter in an amazing way! Immediately upon my return, from South Sudan, I began public ministry, overseeing a congregation of men and women at a residential complex for active seniors.

The very next year, on November 1, 2009 (my spiritual birthday), God did another amazing thing. In His special timing, I was commissioned as a Minister of the Gospel of Jesus Christ! The first time, I was born into the Kingdom of God; now, I was promoted into the service of God: the most holy work of preaching The Gospel of Jesus Christ!

Finally, in May of 2011, God saw fit that I should be ordained into the ministry. I have a God-given passion for not only inner healing–emotional and spiritual reconciliation–but also to reach the lost with the ministry and message of reconciliation, as well as to raise up an end-time army of *Ambassadors for Christ*, who prepare **The Way** of the Lord: **The Way Makers!**

The Lord spoke deeply to my heart and began to show me that it was time to prepare for the fire–the fire of His Spirit to come for the next phase of service. In order for that to happen, I have to share His message with you. This is the third and final trimester. There is much pressure on my womb; however, amidst the struggle and uncertainty, with overcoming faith, I hear God saying to me, "PUSH, PUSH, PUSH!" In humble obedience, I declare God's clarion call to you, future *Ambassador of Christ*, to carry the message and ministry of reconciliation: **Be reconciled to God!**

Introduction

Prophecy

"A voice of **one** calling: 'In the desert prepare the way for the Lord; make straight in the wilderness a highway for our God'" (Isa. 40:3, NIV, emphasis added).

"I will send my messenger, who will prepare the way before me. Then suddenly the Lord you are seeking will come to His temple; the messenger of the covenant, whom you desire will come, says the Lord Almighty" (Mal. 3:1, NIV).

Fulfillment

"In those days John the Baptist came, preaching in the Desert of Judea and saying, 'Repent, for the kingdom of heaven is near.' This is He who was spoken of through the prophet Isaiah: "A voice of **one** calling in the desert, 'Prepare the way for the Lord, make straight paths for Him'" (Matt. 3:1-3, NIV, emphasis added).

We are, indeed, living in the last days, approaching the return of our Lord and Savior Jesus Christ. Nation rising against nation in wars and rumors of wars; political conflicts; terrorism; natural disasters like the Tsunami and Hurricane Katrina; decadent moral decay and the insatiable movement away from Godly influence all speak of the culmination of this dispensation. On this backdrop, who will usher in the return of Jesus, the soon-coming King, with one voice, one mind, and one heart? There is **one** voice predestined to answer the call: The Body of Christ, His unified Bride. The Bride must make Herself ready! God is raising up a unified voice to announce, "Here's the bridegroom! Come out to meet him!" (Matt. 25:6, NIV).

The Way Makers have the noble responsibility of Kingdom preparation. What does it mean to *prepare*? Webster's Dictionary says: "to make (someone or something) ready for some activity, purpose or use; to make or create (an environment) that is ready; to establish an environment for something to take place; to make ready beforehand for some purpose, use or activity; to put in a proper state of mind. Other definitions are:

Introduction

to make room for; to make a pathway; to establish order." We play a strategic role in preparing for the end-time ingathering of the harvest. "...The harvest is plentiful but the workers are few. Ask the Lord of the harvest, therefore, to send out workers into his harvest field" (Matt. 9:37-38, Luke 10:2, NIV). There can be no ingathering without laborers; clearly, we do not have enough! We need to be equipped and *prepared* for that role spiritually, emotionally, and physically.

Further, there can be no harvest without first sowing seed and establishing structure to receive the anticipated harvest. The Word of God is our seed and it needs to be spoken, written, and responded to for the Kingdom. Faith comes by hearing, and hearing by the Word of God. Yet how can we hear unless there is a preacher?

I have received a mandate from the Lord to equip, empower, and inspire leaders in ministry and the marketplace to have Kingdom influence. This book lays out a two-part strategy for making preparation for the return of our Lord Jesus Christ:

Part One – *Preparing The Way of the Lord: In the Life of a Way Maker*. Leaders must be equipped to effectively bring in the harvest.

There is "[the] voice of one calling in the wilderness: **prepare ye the way of the Lord**, make straight in the desert a highway for our God" (Isaiah 40:3, emphasis added, Mal. 3:1, Matt. 3:1-3). Take notice of the fact that in this translation, the scriptures say, "prepare ye;" in other words, **we** prepare. It is **our** responsibility to prepare! We will examine the life of John the Baptist, who is the biblical example of a Way Maker. Specifically from the passage of John 1:19-42, we will examine:

- The Making of a Way Maker – Luke 1:16-17
- The Call of the Way Maker – Mal. 3:1
- The Role of the Way Maker – Luke 3:16
- The Message of the Way Maker – Matthew 3
- The Mission of the Way Maker – Luke 1:76-77
- The Prayer of the Way Maker
- The Commissioning of the Way Maker

Part Two – *Preparing The Way of the Lord: In the House of the Lord*. Where there is confusion (disorder), there is every evil work. Every organization must have in place a system of order: non-profits; businesses; even ministries and Churches. There is an anointing of order and structure that bears witness of the Kingdom of

Introduction

God, draws others to Christ, and provides a spiritually healthy environment in which we can grow and flourish.

This book is an "all call" to you and I, who have ears to hear, and are ready to respond in the end-time hour. God has called me to sound the alarm and to equip, admonish, and encourage us, as together we respond in obedience to preach The Gospel of Jesus Christ!

PART ONE

**PREPARING THE WAY OF THE LORD:
IN THE LIFE OF A WAY MAKER**

The Making of a Way Maker

"But the angel said to him: "Do not be afraid, Zechariah; your prayer has been heard. Your wife Elizabeth will bear you a son, and you are to call him John. He will be a joy and delight to you, and many will rejoice because of his birth, for he will be great in the sight of the Lord. He is never to take wine or other fermented drink, and he will be filled with the Holy Spirit even before he is born. He will bring back many of the people of Israel to the Lord their God. And he will go on before the Lord, in the spirit and power of Elijah, to turn the hearts of the parents to their children and the disobedient to the wisdom of the righteous—to make ready a people prepared for the Lord." Luke 1:13-17

John the Baptist was a child of promise: his birth and ministry were foretold by the prophets Isaiah (40:3) and Malachi (3:1). It was prophesied that John the Baptist would not only be the forerunner of the Messiah's second return, but God fulfills an even greater purpose: John the Baptist actually becomes the bridge between the Old Testament and the New Testament!

Like their ancestors, God sent an angel to Zachariah and Elizabeth, a couple of the priestly line of Aaron, who walked upright and blameless before the Lord. Yet Elizabeth was barren and far advanced in years. In the fullness of time, God sent the angel Gabriel to Zachariah with an astounding message: his prayers had been answered! His wife, Elizabeth, would bear him a son and he was to be called "John", which means "God is favorable".

Now Mary and Elizabeth were relatives, and Elizabeth was already six months pregnant when Mary came to visit her. When Elizabeth heard Mary's greeting, her baby leapt in her womb! The scriptures say that John was filled with the Holy Spirit in his mother's womb. I believe John knew Jesus, by his spirit, from that moment on. I believe the seed of destiny was planted and nurtured all through his childhood by his father, Zachariah, who prophesied at birth:

"And you, my child, will be called a prophet of the Most High; for you will go on before the Lord to prepare the way for him..." (Luke 1:76)

Like Jesus, we don't know a lot about the details of John's childhood, but we know he was the son of priestly parents, which means he was raised and educated according to Jewish custom. Luke 1:80 says, "And the child grew and became strong in spirit; and he lived in the wilderness until he appeared publicly to Israel." Like Jesus, he learned obedience through the things he suffered, and his preparation for ministry took place in the wilderness of the desert.

Yes, God had big plans for John the Baptist! Our text tells us that he was going to be a great prophet, and he would return many who were lost back to Israel. *This is the most significant aspect of John's ministry, and it will prove to be a central part of our ministry as Way Makers.* I believe John knew the call of God on his life, and he spent many years preparing to be about his Father's business. Later in this chapter, we will look at the process of preparation in John's life and how it relates to our preparation as a Way Maker.

John was a student of the scriptures. When the priests and Levites asked him, "Who are you?" he replied with Isaiah's prophecy, "I am the voice of one calling in the wilderness: 'Make straight the way of the Lord.'" (John 1:23; Isa. 40:3) When they asked him, "Why then do you baptize if you are not the Messiah, nor Elijah, nor the Prophet?" he told them that he baptizes with water, but there was a greater coming after him, whom even he was unworthy. John was unwavering in his faith, his identity and what he was called to do. As we continue to explore what it means to be a Way Maker, after the order of John the Baptist we, too, must first be confident and unwavering in what we believe.

Know What You Believe

There was a brief moment, while John the Baptist was in prison, that he began to question whether or not Jesus was the Messiah. (John 7:19-23) Things took a turn for the worse and it caused John to stumble, to be offended. The same will happen to us: there will be times when we will wonder why we were called or even if we were ever called! When those times come, we must know what we believe and be able to articulate it to those who are searching for answers.

We must be absolutely convinced in our own hearts that Jesus Christ is the Son of God, who He died for your sins, and rose again on the third day (2 Cor. 4:13-14). You and I must be absolutely convinced that the Word of God is infallible and written under the inspiration of the Holy Spirit. We cannot let outward appearances influence our ability to obey God in this regard. We must learn to speak the truth in love–the love of Christ.

What do you believe about:

- God and The Divine Trinity – Father, Son, and Holy Spirit?
- Man's Sin – The Fall of Man; God's Provision for Salvation; Our Free Will?

- Jesus Christ – The Atonement for our Sins; The Word Made Flesh; His Death, Burial, and Resurrection?
- Eternal Life – What is salvation? What is conversion?
- The Holy Spirit – The Third Person of the Godhead; Our Seal of Redemption; His Ministry?
- The Bible – The Infallible Word of God; Its Authorship?
- Christ's Return?
- Eternity vs. Hell – Is there a difference?

It is vitally important that you are knowledgeable about the basic tenants of your faith. It is also wise to have a basic understanding of other religious beliefs in order for you to be a more effective *Ambassador of Christ*.

A Season of Preparation

Regarding life in the Kingdom: everything is a *process*; there is no such thing as *instant success* or *overnight fame*. Between the initial call and the manifestation of the call, lies *the process* (also referred to as the *season of preparation*). Preparation is a vital part of the process. If you find yourself on the other side without thoroughly going through the process, you are probably in for some rough times ahead. Although it is often painful and it can be lengthy–depending on the calling–of this, you can be sure: preparation is absolutely necessary!

✣ Preparation **makes you more sensitive to God and your Kingdom purpose**. During this season, you should diligently seek the face of God to find out what His good, perfect and, acceptable will is for your life. He will guide you step by step. These steps may or may not be tangible actions, but rather surrendering of your will, humility of spirit, or an attitude of gratitude. Whatever it is, God who sees in secret will reward you openly. The more you seek Him, the more sensitive you become to His voice and leading.

- ❖ Preparation **purifies, cleanses, and refines**. God cares more about your character than your comfort. He has begun a good work in you and will see it through to completion. This is the season of purification of motives; deliverance from bad habits; and sanctification and enlarging our faith (Psalms 31:10, 119:113, Isa. 54:2, Matt. 5:8).
- ❖ Preparation **enlarges your capacity to receive from God**. The scriptures say, open your mouth wide and He will fill it! (paraphrase)
- ❖ Preparation **helps to bring focus for new things–to receive with a fresh perspective**. You begin to recognize and focus on those things that are eternal, rather than the things of earth (Colossians 3:2). You learn to depend on Him–only. You learn that you can put your trust in Him and that He will never let you be ashamed (Psalm 34:5, Isa. 45:22).
- ❖ Preparation **enables you to bear fruit** (John 15). When you spend time abiding in the Word of God, you are nourished, built up, and equipped to do all things in Christ Jesus. Your ministry is of no effect when you try to accomplish Kingdom work in your own strength. Apart from Him, you can do nothing.

John the Baptist prepared for his ministry in the desert–not in comfort or luxury; just simple living with basic provision. There is something about the desert that makes it the ideal environment to encounter God. Even more significant is the fact that every leader God calls goes through the same process. Here are some characteristics of what life may look like in the desert:

- In the desert, there are no distractions.
- You listen more intently to God.
- It is a time when God pulls you aside to deal with your issues.
- It is an intense time of fellowship and intimacy with God.
- You become more aware of your dependency on God.
- It is usually a place of discomfort, due to the lack of, or very minimal, resources.

God is calling you (and the greater Body of Christ) to be the voice of **one** crying out to those still lost in the world. They are hungry, searching for answers to their dilemmas, and they ***will*** listen! Nonetheless, it depends on whether or not **you** are ready, based on how well you listened and learned while, personally, in the desert. If you are in a desert place now, know that your deliverance is dependent upon your level of submission to the process–*now*.

Enduring the Cross

"Therefore, since we are surrounded by such a great cloud of witnesses, let us throw off everything that hinders and the sin that so easily entangles. And let us run with perseverance the race marked out for us, fixing our eyes on Jesus, the pioneer and perfecter of faith. For the joy set before him he endured the cross, scorning its shame, and sat down at the right hand of the throne of God. Consider him who endured such opposition from sinners, so that you will not grow weary and lose heart.

Endure hardship as discipline; God is treating you as his children. For what children are not disciplined by their father? If you are not disciplined—and everyone undergoes discipline—then you are not legitimate, not true sons and daughters at all. Moreover, we have all had human fathers who disciplined us and we respected them for it. How much more should we submit to the Father of spirits and live! They disciplined us for a little while as they thought best; but God disciplines us for our good, in order that we may share in his holiness. No discipline seems pleasant at the time, but painful. Later on, however, it produces a harvest of righteousness and peace for those who have been trained by it." (Hebrews 12:1-3, 12:7-11, NIV)

We all have a calling on our lives. Our success in making it to the finish line largely depends upon our ability to *endure*. The word *"endure"* means, "to hold up under pain and fatigue; to tolerate; to continue; to last; to bear pain without flinching."

There are many of us, who recognize the call of God on our lives, but are not willing to allow Him to shape us into the man or woman we are destined to become from the foundation of the world. In Matt. 16:24, "...Jesus unto his disciples, 'if any man will come after Me, let him deny himself, and take up his cross, and follow me.'"

"Enduring the Cross," means to hold up under the suffering, pain and hardship, and even death (to self) for the sake of Jesus Christ.

"That I may know Him, and the *power* of His resurrection, and the *fellowship of His sufferings*, being made conformable unto His death" (Phil. 3:10, emphasis added). What is meant by the *fellowship of His sufferings*? The word "*fellowship*" is defined as a relationship in which parties hold something in common; a familiar interaction. We cannot "know God," i.e., be in *fellowship* with Him, unless we, through Jesus Christ, hold the thoughts, feelings and purposes of His heart.

I have been touched with the feelings of His infirmity. I have endured false accusations, being the subject of controversy, being judged and misunderstood, treated unfairly, lied to, betrayed, and disrespected. I have experienced opposition that produced enormous pressure, discomfort, and stress. And yet, I have watched God defend my cause, vindicate me, and reposition me by His grace. We (Jesus and I) have *fellowship* with each other through **suffering**.

But *fellowship* is not found just in the sharing of purposes, passions and, preferences; it is also the sharing of joys and sorrows, fellowship, and conflict. What makes Jesus' resurrection so powerful is the **suffering** that precedes it! Before there is resurrection, there is suffering; we **cannot** have one without the other.

As I said earlier, I was met with so much opposition, to the point that I felt like I was taking the greatest spiritual test of my inner life. God was calling me to **deny myself, take up my cross, and follow Him**. That meant dying to my agenda, to being right, to being included, to my perceived rights, to my reputation, to my control, to the temptation to defend myself, and refrain from quitting. The struggle was enormous! In my distress, I cried out to the Lord. God spoke to me through His Word and asked, "***If I could endure all of that for you, can you not endure this for Me?***" (Heb. 12:2-3). Needless to say, I dissolved into a puddle of tears. My greatest desire was (and still is) to please Him and be found trustworthy and faithful to stay the course He'd set before me. I did not want to let Him down.

In Heb. 4:15-16, the writer says, "For we do not have a high priest who is unable to ***empathize*** with our weaknesses, but we have one who has been tempted in every way, just as we are—yet he did not sin. Let us then approach God's throne of grace with confidence, so that we may receive mercy and find grace to help us in our time of need" (NIV, emphasis added). However, the question is: are we willing to *empathize* with His sufferings? *So I asked God to help me to run the race marked out for me.* What I have come to understand is that there are three things required to run with patience the race marked out for you and I:

- **Focus**
- Patience
- Endurance

As we run this race, we are not to look at the crowd in the stands or the cheerleaders on the sidelines. No! Our eyes are always on **the prize, the finish line, or the joy that is set before us.** Therefore, **to keep sharp focus**, we must **run our race looking unto Jesus**, the author and finisher of our faith (Heb. 12:1-3).

To keep our focus on God, we **must** stay in His Word; keeping our eyes on that which is unseen, not on what we see in the natural. If we focus on our circumstances, we will faint. Whenever we stop looking at Him, we will lose our joy and become full of anxiety and fear. Just like Peter, who began to sink, once he took his eyes off of Jesus, focusing on the wind and waves. When we release all to Him, our joy and peace will always come back. We must stay close to God; continuously guarding our hearts and our tongues.

A great and effectual door is open unto us; yet, there are many adversaries (1 Cor. 16:9). Still, none are as dangerous and life threatening as the enemies of our soul: pride, worry, fear, inflexibility, selfish ambition, control, and self-reliance. These are the sins that can and will so easily beset us, causing you and I to lose our focus. Once that happens, we cannot **see** what is in front of us and we cannot **hear** the voice behind us saying, "This is the way; walk in it" (Isa. 30:21b).

Second, we must understand and submit to being trained and disciplined by the process: our *endurance training*. God disciplines those He loves. In order for us to be equipped, we must submit to *endurance training*. No discipline seems pleasant at the time. And we certainly do not see the benefit of it when we are going through it (Heb. 12:7-11). For our momentary yet light afflictions work for us a far more exceeding and eternal weight of glory!

Finally, we cannot be ignorant of the devil's devices; we have an adversary whose sole purpose in life is to steal, kill, and destroy us plus our God-given callings. He is the father of lies and the accuser of the brethren. We defeat him when we renew our minds with the Truth of God's Word.

- Focus
- **Patience**
- Endurance

"My brethren, count it all joy when ye fall into divers temptations; Knowing this, that the trying of your faith works patience. But let patience have her perfect work, that ye may be perfect and entire, wanting nothing" (Heb. 10:35-39, James 1:2-4, 1 Peter 4:12-16).

We should not think it strange when diverse trials and tribulations come our way. It is for our equipping. Count it all joy. Let patience have its perfect work. For we have need of patience. God wants us to be equipped, not lacking in any area. We must stay in the race and cultivate the attitude that Paul had when he said, "**I press toward the mark for the prize of the high calling of God in Christ Jesus**" (Phil. 3:14, emphasis added).

The race is not won by the swift; it is won by those of us who *endure* to the end. Therefore, we cannot cast away our confidence for it has great recompense of reward. And after we have suffered a while, He will strengthen, establish, and settle us.

Putting it into Practice

- Focus
- Patience
- **Endurance**

Jesus "***endured the cross***..." (Heb. 12:1-4). What did Jesus do during His race? Before and after ministry, Jesus always went away, alone, to pray in a solitary place. He replenished Himself spiritually and physically.

We must pace ourselves with spiritual disciplines:
- **_Prayer and Quiet Time_**. Casting all our cares upon Him, because He cares for us.
- **_Beware of distractions_**. Resist getting entangled in family matters, office politics, our past, the demands of others and busyness. **Example:** Jesus did not come to Lazarus until it was time; He did not go to Jerusalem until it was time.
- **_Guarding our hearts_** and **_thought life_**. Be slow to speak, slow to anger, and quick to forgive. **Example:** "But Jesus would not entrust himself to them, for he knew all men" (John 2:24). "Casting down imaginations, and every high thing that exalts itself against the knowledge of God, and bringing into captivity every thought to the obedience of Christ" (2 Cor. 10:5).
- **_Declaring the Word_**–"_It is written..._" Jesus declared who He is: "I am The Bread of Life;" "I am Living Water;" "I am The Resurrection and the Life;" "I am The Good Shepherd;" etc. We make declarations over our lives: "I am a Child of God;" "I am more than a conqueror;" "I am an heir of God and joint heir with Jesus Christ;" "I shall

live and not die, to declare the Word of the Lord."
- ***Compassion**–"...**Father, forgive them for they know not what they do**...*" (Luke 23:24) It was His long-suffering and compassion that helped Him to endure to the very end. I believe this is what is meant by *the passion* of Jesus Christ.

Do Not Expect Ease All the Time

We are being prepared for that which Christ has apprehended us: "For we are his workmanship, created in Christ Jesus unto good works, which God hath before ordained that we should walk in them" (Ephesians 2:10). Often times, those *good works* are carried out in dangerous times and in uncomfortable places. We are being prepared to bring in the final ingathering of souls.

Matt. 4:1-3 says: "Then was Jesus led up of the Spirit into the wilderness to be tempted of the devil. And when he had fasted forty days and forty nights, he was afterward hungered. And when the tempter came to him, he said, 'If thou be the Son of God, command that these stones be made bread.'"

Jesus comes out of the wilderness full of power and the Holy Spirit. The scriptures say a great light shown in a dark place. God always sends us, His light, into dark places. Our light must shine brighter than ever in a lost, dark world. How do we know when our light is shining? Sometimes God will let us know in a supernatural way; one time, He showed me—on the most unassuming day!

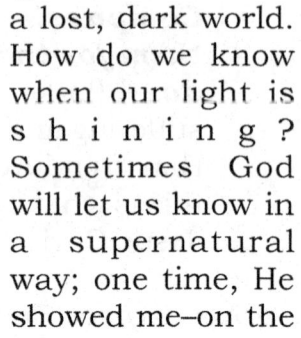

> **God always sends us, His light, into dark places.**

My husband and I went out to dinner on "date night." Since we chose a different restaurant, I slowly approached the buffet; looking for the food items I would like the most. As I strolled from one counter to the other, a woman approached me, put her hand on my arm, and said:

"You are a woman of God aren't you?" I had never seen her before!

"Yes, I am," I responded warmly.

"I could tell there was something different about you," she replied.

I smiled, marveling that God saw me. **Me**! After I finally picked up a plate and started to serve myself, she came back to me and said, "Do not let your light go out. Never let your light go out!" She was so emphatic that I processed her sense of urgency as a warning that something, someone, or a future situation in my life had the potential of dimming – or snuffing out – my light.

God had revealed to me that my light was shining! Later I came to understand, it was not something or someone outside of myself. It was me: I was in danger of letting my light go out if I did not continue in the Word of God, prayer, praise and worship.

The Whole Armor of God

When we are in a dark place, we must always put on the whole armor of God, as outlined in Ephesians 6:11-18. We fight with the weapons of our warfare: the Word of God, prayer, praise and worship. In these last days, we must be able to stand against the wiles of the devil. God cannot use a **spiritual pushover**. We are admonished not to be ignorant of the devil's devices: discouragement, distractions, disappointments, intimidation, etc. Often, the most significant way to discern if our light is shining is by the level of opposition we face. Jesus came to His own, but His own did not even recognize nor receive Him (John 1:10-11).

Valuable Lessons

On this journey, of cultivating focus, patience, and endurance, we must learn two valuable lessons in: humility and the freedom of choice.

First, in order to *endure* and to bear fruit in suffering, we need true, God-given

humility. 1 Peter 5:5-7 states, "...God opposes the proud, but *gives grace to the humble*. Humble yourselves, therefore, under God's mighty hand, that he may lift you up in due time. Cast all your anxiety on him because he cares for you" (NIV, emphasis added).

The second is about **choices**. Every time we chose to obey God, it hurts – sometimes it really hurts. Though we could do it our way, which seems less painful, it probably will abort our race to our individual (and corporate) destiny. Beloved, we need to watch the choices that we make. Paul did not mince words when he said, "Whoever sows to please their flesh, from the flesh will reap destruction; whoever sows to please the Spirit, from the Spirit will reap eternal life" (Galatians 6:8). Choose ***life***!

We may not realize it now, but *fruitful suffering* yields a harvest of *righteousness, peace,* and *holiness* if we do not faint. Like Jesus, we will learn obedience through the things we suffer; like Paul, we will come to know Him in the *power* of His resurrection and the "...*fellowship of His sufferings*..." (Phil. 3:10, emphasis added).

> **The race is not won by the swift; it is won by those of us who endure to the end.**

The Making of a Way Maker

The race is not won by the swift; it is won by those of us who endure to the end. "Now may the God of peace, who through the blood of the eternal covenant brought back from the dead our Lord Jesus, that great Shepherd of the sheep, equip you with everything good for doing his will, and may he work in us what is pleasing to him, through Jesus Christ, to whom be glory forever and ever. Amen." (Heb. 13:20-21 NIV).

Healing before Ministry

Every week, I participate in a business and ministry conference call, where I, and several women, share on answering the leading of God in our lives in the arenas of business and ministry. We share for the purpose of edification and encouragement. During one call, we talked about the enemies of our soul that kept us from responding in obedience, including: fear, intimidation, shame, poor self-esteem or self-image, fear of man, rejection, or abandonment–and how they manifest themselves in self-destructive ways in our lives. When the moderator gave the introduction and started the conversation, she asked us to begin to share some of the issues we had encountered and what we did in response. There was a pregnant pause because, of course, no one wanted to be the *first* to share–including me! However, during that moment of silence, the Holy Spirit got on my case.

He said, "Stop! Stop holding back! Stop waiting for someone else to speak up. You have something to share and they need to hear it!" Had this silent conversation been reenacted, it would look like someone pushing me onto a theater stage against my will, telling me to get out there and speak up! The truth is, I do have a testimony; and I need to share it.

The Making of a Way Maker

Someone once told me that we are as sick as our secrets bottled up inside of us. When God has done a work in our lives–in other words, we have a testimony–but we do not share it, it can make us sick–spiritually! We overcome by the Blood of the Lamb and the word of our testimony (Rev. 12:11). So, we have to open our mouths and **share**! Giving voice to the glorious work of God is the key to living victorious lives! I believe it grieves the heart of God when He does something wonderful and supernatural for us – something we could not do for ourselves – and we hide it out of fear: fear of man, fear of what people will think, or because we want to hide behind a superficial façade. If we cannot walk in transparency, humility, and authenticity, we will never bring the lost to Christ. In fact, **the word of my testimony** compelled me to write this book. If I want to reach the lost, the victories of God in my walk must be shared. Anything less, is blatant disobedience and makes my ministry of no effect.

So I opened my mouth and began to share. As the words came out, I wondered if those same fears kept me from even completing this book sooner. Yes, there were a few times when legitimate reasons required I shift my focus and attention elsewhere; rarely does the life of a writer flow without interruption. Still, something in my heart told me that it was true: fear had held me captive. So as I write this segment, I am filled with gratitude, for I see how far Jesus has brought me. I am now at a place in my journey where I am more concerned about living a life of obedience and pleasing God – and that desire is stronger than my fears! Hallelujah!

It is my prayer that as I share with you my journey to wholeness, you will: be encouraged and set free in some areas; realize that you are not alone; know that God sees you; and, He is working in you both to will and to do what pleases Him. It does not happen all at once; in fact, wholeness is a life-long process. However, as you begin to acknowledge areas of weakness (God will put His finger on them), you will begin to experience change and growth; but you must yield to the process. You might wonder, "How will I know what God is putting His finger on?" Wonderful question! You will know by the area(s) where you are experiencing the most pain and struggle. Look at it. Allow God to look at it. Now agree with God and submit to the work of The Holy Spirit.

Even as God begins to build our spiritual muscles through His Word, He will also begin a work of inner healing as we grow and mature. He edifies, sanctifies, and purifies us from the inside out. Many ministries have fallen prey to destruction because the process of inner healing did not have its perfect work. To skip this process, means we run the risk of aborting our destiny altogether. **This is**

serious business; souls are hanging in the balance. Therefore, we must reach a certain level of emotional and spiritual health in order to fulfill our end-time assignment. Yes, this is a life-long process; still, we go from glory to glory in our walk with God.

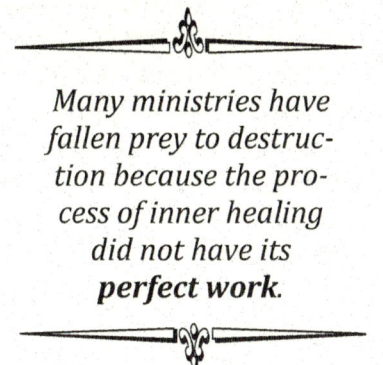

*Many ministries have fallen prey to destruction because the process of inner healing did not have its **perfect work**.*

Clearing Away the Stones

The Kingdom of God must first come inside us. When we usher in His presence in our own lives, our lights will so shine that others will see our good works and glorify our Father in heaven. Revival always takes place in us first. When the Word of God is preached, it is first preached to the speaker. It must first be made flesh in our own lives. In 1 Cor. 9:27, Paul says, "But I keep under my body, and bring it into subjection: lest that by any means, when I have preached to others, I myself should be a castaway."

We must clear out the soil of our hearts, removing the stones of: idolatry, pride, selfish ambition, jealousy, covetousness, addictions, anger, uncleanness, adultery, disobedience, and unforgiveness (Isa. 57:14, 62:10, Jer. 18:15, Romans 12).

The Way Makers

In this section, we will explore the topic of inner healing as a critically important condition to being effective *Ambassadors of Christ*. So, how do we first experience reconciliation in our own lives? The important thing we must realize is: reconciliation is a process of renouncing the lies of the enemy and declaring the truth of God's Word. The prerequisites are a broken and contrite spirit–in other words, **humility**–and the **Word of God**, which is our weapon of choice.

Biblical Leaders

Moses – Moses had an extremely volatile anger problem. His inability to manage his emotions cost him his leadership role and personally ushering the Nation of Israel into the Promised Land (Numbers 20:10-12). What a bitter pill to swallow! After being chosen by God to deliver His people, Moses ended up forfeiting the blessing of entering into God's rest. Moses is a perfect example of the ripple effect of what one small, yet costly, mistake looks like when we are emotionally unhealthy leaders.

King Saul – Jealousy cost King Saul the throne of Israel (1 Samuel 18:7-9). He was so consumed with jealousy for David that he embarked on a relentless pursuit to kill him. In the end, King Saul forfeited the throne because of his disobedience of the Word of God. Moreover, he demonstrated a lack of character by blaming the men under his leadership for taking the spoils; adding insult to injury, he lied about it to the Prophet Samuel's face! (1 Samuel 15) Samuel refusing to accompany him was tantamount to God removing His grace and anointing from King Saul's life. When the Presence of God leaves, we are in big trouble.

Paul – He said, "I am the least of all the apostles, and do not even deserve to be called an apostle" (Acts 9:1-31, 1 Cor. 15:1-11). Initially, Paul had a sincere hatred for Christians. God had to supernaturally transform him in order to use him to preach to the Gentiles–the people outside of his race and culture. More than anything, Paul was in need of healing. We can see his brokenness and shame in the scripture quoted earlier. How was he going to be effective with this attitude of the heart? How was he going to embrace the call of God on his life?

Paul went to Arabia for period of three years and stayed there before he went to be with some of the other apostles. During his time in the desert, God did a deep inner healing in Paul – a healing that had to take place in order for him to fulfill his God-given purpose and calling to the Gentiles.

One of the greatest discoveries in my spiritual growth was identifying and acknowledging that I struggled with co-dependency. I want to take some time to share a little about co-dependency and then define it in the hopes that the "light bulb" will turn on. Do not feel ashamed. Not only is this character flaw pervasive, but millions of people, ministers, pastors and leaders, especially women, suffer under the weight of it – some even to the point of death.

On the Road to Recovery

One of our primary goals as *Ambassadors for Christ* has to be cultivating **emotional and spiritual health**. In other words, we strive to be whole in our emotions as well as our spiritual life. To do that means we allow God to deal with those issues or areas of constant struggle. Some include: defensiveness every time someone asks us about our work; resentment that rises up when we are asked for the twentieth time to give Mr. Smith a ride to church; and, finally, the overwhelming fear and intimidation every time we have to interact with certain people we believe are superior to us.

There are many more examples we could add to the list. Every time we experience inner conflict, it is sign that something is wrong and God wants to deal with it – if we will let Him. He wants to bring the inner healing necessary for us to be whole and effective in our witness and ministry. However, God does not, nor should we expect for Him to, deal with all of our struggles at one time–it would utterly destroy us! We will know the hierarchy of what God wants to deal with by the level of emotional struggle and discomfort we experience. God has a way of putting His finger on the right struggle and, if we are sensitive to the promptings of the Holy Spirit, we will know when God is speaking to us about it. We need to listen and submit to the process.

> *It is impossible to be spiritually mature, but emotionally immature. ("Emotionally Healthy Spirituality"*

If we are to be effective in our personal witness and discipling of others, then it is extremely important, vital – even crucial – that we become emotionally healthy Christians. It is impossible to be spiritually mature, but emotionally immature. ("Emotionally Healthy Spirituality" by Peter Scazzero)[1]

The Healing Process

- Humility
- Confession
- Forgiveness–offer and receive
- Reconciliation–newness of life

In order for us to be effective ministers of reconciliation, we must first be reconciled to God in our own lives. The well-known expression, **wounded people wound people,** is absolutely true. Unintentionally, we will try to minister life from a position of weakness, rather than a position of strength.

To that end, we need to appropriate emotional healing for ourselves through prayer, allowing the Spirit of God to heal and restore. To accomplish this we will need:

- An **attitude of humility**–recognizing our own moral and emotional deficits. We ask God to show us our stones.
- **Confession**– To appropriate healing involves more than just confessing our sins; it is walking in deliverance by replacing the lies of the enemy with declaration of the truth of God's Word.
- Seek healing through forgiveness. We forgive every person and offense, allowing the Holy Spirit to comfort us, knowing that He is our defense and advocate. Vengeance belongs to the Lord! The most important part of this process is to **forgive yourself**. Forgive yourself because everyone makes mistakes. What is most important is that you learn from those mistakes and become a better, stronger person. The truth is, real growth only comes by falling and making mistakes. Just because you did not think, say or do everything right, does not make you a failure. We learn and we grow. Forgive yourself.
- The ministry of reconciliation and walking in newness of life. We have been reconciled by faith and restored to communion with God. Every day,

we cultivate an intimate relationship with Him and with others.

The Word of God, prayer as well as praise and worship are our weapons of choice to combat the obstacles strategically placed by the devil to effectively hinder our ministry–if not addressed.

Declarations for Deliverance

Say these declarations, out loud, every day:
- I am delivered from the power of darkness. (Col. 1:13)
- I am healed by the stripes of Jesus Christ. (1 Peter 2:24)
- I am free! (John 8:36)
- I am loved with an everlasting love. (Jer. 31:3)
- I am complete in Christ. (Col. 2:10)
- I am fit to partake of His inheritance. (Col. 1:12)
- I am dead to sin. (Romans 6:2)
- I am alive to God. (Romans 6:11)
- I am holy, without blame, and free from accusation. (Col. 1:22)
- I have peace with God. (Romans 5:1)
- I am more than a conqueror. (Romans 8:37)
- Nothing can separate me from the love of God. (Romans 8:38-39)

A Personal Testimony

A huge part of my preparation for ministry was in the area of inner healing. Aside from the time spent studying the Word of God and taking courses – studying in order to show myself approved is required in the process – the rest was all the inner working of the Holy Spirit. So, allow me to share two testimonies on my road to inner healing and what I discovered along the way.

The Old Me

My early childhood was filled with laughter and fun-filled days playing with all of my cousins. My mother had three sisters and they all lived on the same street. I remember many summers, holidays and special Christmases being surrounded by my family. We never had much; in fact, we were poor, but as children, we never knew it! We always had new clothes and were able to take advantage of lots of school activities. My mother instilled in me a love books and reading at a very early age. She taught me all forms of needlework from crocheting to latch-hooking rugs. Those were my favorite past times. When I wasn't out riding my bike or jumping double-dutch, you would find me in my room "playing teacher" or reading a book. I spent a lot of time alone, even as a child.

Despite those fond memories, my adolescent and teen years were marked by broken relationships, single parenthood, and emotional dysfunction. As the oldest of three (one brother, two years younger; one sister, ten years younger), I grew up under the weight of rejection, abandonment, low self-esteem, and insecurity. My mother was always telling me: "You're a pain in the ass." When I was hurt by something, she would say, "Oh hush (or shut up); it's not that bad. So what? Stop making such a big deal!" Oh, and this was her all-time favorite: "You talk too much!" Maybe I did; however, later on in life, her constant declaration would prove to be a hindrance in fulfilling my calling as a "Messenger of God." Ironically, it is most interesting that my mother would name me, Angela, which means "Messenger of God," and then never miss an opportunity to tell me that I talked too much!

> *Ironically, it is most interesting that my mother would name me, Angela, which means "Messenger of God," and then never miss an opportunity to tell me that I talked too much!*

The Making of a Way Maker

When my sister was born, my responsibilities exponentially increased. My mother was employed by the United States Postal Service and worked the graveyard shift for a long time. When I graduated from high school, she switched to the 3:00 p.m. to 11:00 p.m. shift. Therefore, the responsibility of caring for my younger brother and sister, every afternoon until midnight, was solely on me: everything from heating up dinner, to homework, to baths, to combing hair, to attending school plays, rides to cheerleading practices, and after-school football games. You name it–I did it. I bought school supplies, clothing, eyeglasses, even contact lenses. I remember having to find a babysitter for my sister one time when I wanted to do something with my friends. On more than one occasion, I had to take her with me. She spent many weekends out with me. Although I did not always mind having her tag along, because I loved her so much, there were a few times when I felt differently.

I basically raised my sister from first grade straight through college. She used to bring her report cards to **me** for signature! Such a relationship made it very difficult for her and I to transition from a "parent/child" relationship to a "sister/sister" relationship while she was in college. I had to **learn how** to be her older sister! It was especially hard for me because my love for her was very maternal. I knew everything about her and could sense when she was crying–even from a block away!

Don't get me wrong. I love my family. I'm really proud of the way my Mom raised the three of us on her own; that was no small fete! She is to be commended. Despite her shortcomings and our dysfunction, she did her very best. It was better than that of other members of our family. That was good enough for me. I just want you to get a sense of what life was like.

Many times, because I was the oldest, I was expected to accept delay in receiving something so that my brother and sister could receive first. For example, my mother promised me a new bike on my birthday. Since my birthday was in January, and my siblings' birthdays were in June, I had to wait until June, so that we would all receive our bikes together. I remember being so hurt by that; it was as if what I wanted or desired did not matter and breaking a promise to me was "no big deal." There were other occasions growing up where I was supposed to expect less so that they could have more.

My mother was a struggling single parent. In her dysfunction, she often made me feel like it was part of my responsibility, as the oldest, to help look after our family's household; that was our dysfunction. I actually began to fill the role of a parent in our household and was expected to readily make that level of sacrifice. I was expected to function in our household like any other adult: paying rent and utilities–even buying my own groceries. I was never allowed to miss a bill payment for any reason. By my late twenties, I began to see the dysfunction for what it had become in my life. Moreover, I was tired of living under the weight of such expectations. So, I began to change and relinquish some of the responsibilities that never should have been mine in the first place. Well, my increased maturity, awareness, and response to the dysfunction caused all kinds of conflict, especially with my mother.

Nothing I did was good enough. If I received a "B" on my report card, she would say I should have gotten an "A." Not to be outdone, my grandmother always called me "fresh" and told my mother she needed to stay home from work and watch me–for I would be the first to get pregnant. Every time there was a dispute between my cousins and myself, I was always made out to be the culprit; if I was not the one that caused the squabble, I should have fixed it. After all, I was the oldest. Sadly, as my sister got older, I noticed she seemed to take on some of the same habits as our mother. It was quite uncommon for both of them to criticize my hairstyle or my clothes – something was always wrong with me. As a result, I was performance-driven my entire childhood

The Way Makers

and young adult life; I strived practically my whole life to prove every one of them wrong! And, I did. From the fifth to the twelfth grade, I was an honor-roll student. I was the first in our family to attend college and I was on the Dean's List the entire time. I never had children, and I was the first to move into my own apartment.

Then a major change occurred in my life. I received the Lord Jesus Christ as my personal savior at the age of twenty-seven. My monumental decision brought further conflict and division between my mother and myself. Keep this in mind: although my mother never accompanied us, we were *required* to go to church *every* Sunday. If we did not want to go to church, we could not go out to play. So, God and church have been a part of my life for as long as I can remember. Yet when I made a serious commitment at the age of twenty-seven, it brought conflict of epic proportions. When I began to work full time in the ministry, my mother would often ask, "When are you going to get a *real* job?" It was only the grace of God that kept me because in those days I did not have the wisdom and maturity to let those spiteful questions and other negative comments roll off my back. I often struggled inwardly with my choices – tormented by always second-guessing myself; nevertheless, all the glory goes to God, who caused me to triumph!

As a young child, I sang in the choir of every church I attended as well as in school. I loved to worship God! When I completely turned my life over to Jesus Christ, as a young woman, I immersed myself in the prayer, worship, home group, and Christian education ministries. No matter where I served, somehow I always ended up in a leadership role, which is how I discovered my ministry and spiritual gifts. After all, I was raised to be a leader (and a teacher of the Word). I was ravenous for the Word of God and many would say that I grew in wisdom and matured quickly in the things of the Kingdom. The truth is, although I was doing well, it was only because inwardly, I was still trying to prove myself worthy of acceptance. I was always trying to please people and would do anything to keep people from being angry with me. I trusted the wrong people and often said the wrong things just to be included and accepted. My goal was to avoid rejection at all costs.

It was not until I was faced with a life threatening illness that the "eyes of my understanding" were opened. Truth be told, I found out who my real friends were when I faced this crisis in my life. Things began to change after that. I began to shift my investment of time and energy away from toxic people. My new attitude was, if you did not value my friendship the way I valued your friendship, then I needed to set boundaries to reflect that. My lowest point was the break-up of a long-term friendship with my very best friend, Pam, and the break-up of a relationship with the man I was seeing at the time (prior to my salvation). After receiving Jesus, an even lower point was the realization of the poor quality of my relationships–as demonstrated when I was fighting for my life in the hospital.

But God is always faithful. He did not leave me dead in my trespasses and sins. He came to my rescue. In 2004 my husband and I moved to Silver Spring, Maryland, so he could begin a new position with the United States Department of Justice. Before I began working, I entered a place called "Sanctuary," for a period of two and a half months. It was a place of transformation. I will share more with you about that life-changing encounter a little later in this book. ***"Sanctuary" is where my inner healing began.***

Now in Maryland, we joined a Church, and few years later, a new ministry started: Celebrate Recovery (C. R.). It is an excellent ministry birthed out of Saddleback Church, under the leadership of Pastor Rick Warren, author of *The Purpose-Driven Life*. After the first year, the overseeing pastor of C. R. approached me about becoming a leader in the ministry. (By this time I had already been ordained as a minister.) At first, I really did not think C. R. was a ministry for me.

"Hurts, Habits, and Hang-ups?" That was not for me! However, I was willing to submit to the process. Boy was I surprised! C. R. was exactly what I needed. God knew it all along! My time in "Sanctuary" was only the beginning. Later I came to realize it was the "breaking up of fallow ground".

My experience in C. R. was nothing short of profound: I was re-introduced to Jesus Christ in a whole new way! He is Jehovah Rapha, my *inner* healer. I had known Him as my physical healer, but to know Him as the One who binds up my broken heart? That was a deeper level of intimacy I had never experienced! My deep desire to please Him and to fulfill His call on my life fueled my desire to walk in emotional and spiritual health. My submission to the process helped me to identify the character defects that were holding me back and keeping me from moving forward in the Will of God. The most significant revelation, and the focus of my recovery, was on: co-dependency (this was the biggest and the most serious revelation). God also touched other areas such as, fear and intimidation; low self-esteem/self-worth; and,

> *I had to grow and mature in many areas before I could accept this fact and cooperate with God.*

insecurity. In the next segment, I share testimonies of my victories in some of these areas. Let me just pause to focus on co-dependency for a moment.

Co-dependency can be defined as an addiction to people, behaviors, or things. Co-dependent people allow themselves to be defined by what others think, feel, and say. Their behavior and thought life are patterned after how other people think, behave, and feel. A few of their characteristics are:

- They often feel like they have no control over their own lives.
- They find it difficult to make decisions.
- They suffer from low self-worth.
- They neglect their own health and well-being for the sake of others.
- They often go through life *reacting* instead of being Spirit-led.
- They feel their self-worth is connected to how well they "perform"–they lead performance-driven lives.
- They act out of guilt or fear of rejection in service to others, rather than acting out of love and genuine concern.

Co-dependent behavior is often camouflaged by seemingly good Christian conduct. After all, are we not supposed to place others before ourselves? Are we not we supposed to look after the interest of others

The Making of a Way Maker

first? The difference is **motive** and **balance**. Because we do not establish healthy boundaries, we find ourselves taking Mr. Smith to church every Sunday, whether we have gas or not; we stay late to clean up after every Women's Ministry meeting even though we are exhausted and have over-taxed our bodies; or, we continue to show up to the book club meeting and suffer through ungodly conversation because we want to be included.

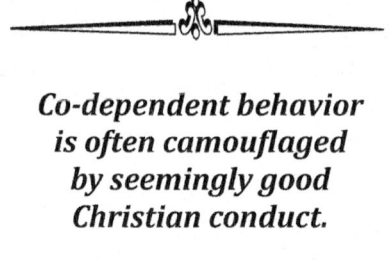

Co-dependent behavior is often camouflaged by seemingly good Christian conduct.

I was over the age of fifty when I made this discovery and it rocked my world! I never knew "it" had a name! For years I struggled under the weight of guilt and condemnation, especially in my family. I did all sorts of things just to gain the approval of others, or to keep them from being angry or disappointed in me. The fact that I *performed* well put me in good stead later in life – but with a very high emotional price.

Once I was able to recognize that "it" was actually **co-dependency**, I began to deal with "it" head on. It was as if the light came on in my soul for the first time! I was no longer walking in darkness and I understood why it took so long: **I had to grow**

and mature in many areas before I could accept this fact and cooperate with God. I was finally there – at the place of healing and deliverance. God did not leave me dead in my trespasses and sins. He came to me and rescued me; my response was humble obedience and surrender. Although the process was hard and emotionally grueling, my God-given strength and wisdom increased tremendously. I have a liberty in my life that energizes me to move forward without fear of rejection.

I am a better minister: the Love of God is shed abroad in my heart from one person to another and it has made my ministry to others more effective. When I minister out of love, I can be free to serve without compulsion or guilt; setting proper boundaries sets my life at a pace that is both God-honoring and self-honoring. Although there were some rough patches in my family relationships, they are still intact and much stronger. When I changed for the better, my family also changed for the better. I believe, individually (though they may not realize it), they have grown and become better people because I began taking care of my own emotional well-being.

In C. R., during Step Four, entitled, "Your Personal Inventory", I identified a specific area of pain and/or conflict and began to evaluate the issues and the people involved; I determined my area of responsibility;

made amends by forgiving or asking for forgiveness; and finally, letting go. I worked through this step three times; it was, by far, the most difficult part for me. Yet, it was also the most revelatory and the most liberating. I did the inner work that produced a new level of emotional wellness.

God birthed a passion in my spirit for inner healing, not just on a personal level, but also for those in any form of leadership – no matter the size of organization. He uniquely equipped me for such a work.

The New Me

I have learned to set and enforce healthy boundaries, even when it is hard or unpopular. This is especially true in family dynamics. I choose my friends far more carefully and I no longer expect the same things from every relationship: each one stands on its own merit and I invest accordingly. I recognize that the wheat must grow with the tares. Everyone is not at the same place in their spiritual or emotional health; I now know enough to recognize what triggers certain emotions in me and how my response affects others.

I know what my responsibilities are, and what they are not. My mood and disposition are no longer dependent on how someone else feels. I have learned to ask for what I need. I can express myself without fear of rejection. I no longer operate from a victim mentality; I have choices. I can choose God's way and walk in victory. I discovered that I am stronger than I think; and by God's grace, I have overcome a lot. I have overcome opposition that would have destroyed someone else. I am more than a conqueror in Christ Jesus! I am able to do whatever He calls me to do; He empowers me to do it. I still struggle in some areas, but I am no longer "looking at their faces!" (Jer. 1:8)

I know who I am, whose I am, and what I am called to be in the Kingdom. I have known God to be my defense. He is my vindication; every weapon formed against me he obliterates. He called, equipped, commissioned, and anointed me. God has my back; I am not afraid of man anymore. Most importantly, I know beyond a shadow of a doubt that God loves me–yes, **me**! I am acceptable to Him.

My walk with God radically changed during this inner transformation. We are closer and our level of intimacy has deepened. I am more dependent on Him because I see myself in light of my weaknesses and recognize that without Him I cannot make it. I cannot reach my full potential without Him. I know that I am worthy because of what He has done for me. My service to others is now born out of great compassion. I now have a sincere burden for inner healing; in fact, I see it as part of my calling because I recognize its importance in developing strong, healthy leaders.

Celebrate Recovery played a most significant role in my emotional and spiritual growth and maturity. As God would have it, I did become a leader and a teacher in C. R. It was one of the most rewarding experiences in my service to the Kingdom. The most fulfilling aspect for me was leading a small group, and coaching and guiding other leaders on their journey to inner wholeness. I continue to share my testimony of my journey to inner healing in public ministry, my blog, and through my writing.

My motives have been purified. Motivation to serve emanates more and more from my love for Him and my desire to please Him, than by what I want, or to please others. In fact, I know that I can never please everyone. My advice: Play to an audience of **One**! Hearing Him quietly whisper, "Well done, faithful servant" is all you and I need to hear.

Beloved, God loves you and I too much to leave us stuck in our trespasses and sins. The scriptures say, "...he who began a good work in you will carry it on to completion until the day of Christ Jesus" (Phil. 1:6, NIV). He will never leave us nor abandon us!

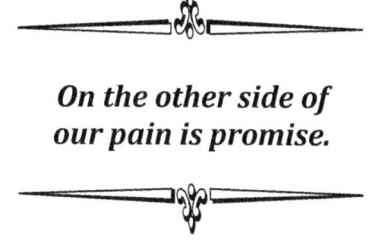

On the other side of our pain is promise.

We must trust Him to bind up our broken hearts–to give us beauty for ashes! *On the other side of our pain is promise.* God will continually bring us through to the other side.

In the next section, I share personal testimonies of actual experiences that I hope will edify, enlighten, and encourage. Remember: we overcome the enemy of our soul by the Blood of the Lamb and the word of our testimony! (Rev. 12:11, NIV)

Deliverance from the Deep-Rooted Spirit of Rejection

Divine Intervention–God Steps into my Dreams

I was in a house or apartment–a different, unrecognizable place–and I heard a knock on the front door. Upon opening the door, I saw my long-time friend, Richard, from my former church: Freedom Christian Bible Fellowship. After entering, he told me he had found something on the back seat of his car. It was a black pouch that looked like an old cigarette case; it was very worn and tattered. In fact, it reminded me of the cigarette case my Aunt Lorraine used to carry. For a moment, I reflected on her life, since she was now in Heaven with the Lord. When I looked inside the case, there was a very thick wad of money. I was shocked–where did it come from?

I heard second knock on the front door. It was another former co-laborer in ministry from the same church. He came in carrying all these new clothes–suits, dresses, blouses, etc. He brought in armful after armful of new clothing, with the tags still attached, and placed them on the sofa.

Then, in walked my mother's oldest sister: my Aunt Carolyn, nicknamed "Cookie." She walked right past me, keeping her focus on going down the hallway to enter my mother's room. I said hello to her but she just ignored me, trying to get past me and arrive at her destination. I kept blocking her path and repeating my greeting. "Hello, Aunt Carolyn." She just cast me aside like I was nobody, like I was not even there; she felt she did not even need acknowledge my presence. Finally, when I blocked her one last time, she responded with a dry "Hi." At that, I unleashed my anger and went on to warn her not to ever treat me that way again–especially in my own house.

In the background, I could hear my mother saying, "Angie, let it go; leave her alone." I thought, "How typical of her; always defending her and my Aunt Lorraine's actions against me. My feelings did not matter. What else was new?" My mother always invalidated my feelings, counting them as being irrational, unrealistic, or somehow not grounded in reality. She was always accepting of my brother and her siblings' behavior–never mine. Nothing I did was ever good enough for her. Even when I succeeded, it was not good enough.

Divine Interpretation

- My mother represented rejection from **birth** (possibly as early as conception).
- My Aunts Lorraine and Cookie represented rejection from **childhood**.

- Richard brought vindication and restoration from rejection in **ministry**.
- The money represented my **spiritual inheritance** in Christ.
- The clothes represented my **robes of righteousness** (I am the righteousness of God in Christ Jesus [2 Cor. 5:21]). These represented the spoils I carried with me from the ministry where I'd served for many years; not in a monetary sense, but in terms of a rich, spiritual inheritance.

God revealed to me the deep root of the spirit of rejection in my life. Once I saw it, I was so hurt. I thought, "I never stood a chance! This has been my life from birth!" God began to show me how this awful spirit was hindering and keeping me from fulfilling my purpose and destiny. That is not all. He began to reveal other areas in my life that triggered emotional rejection. I share them in the hope that you may identify with some or all of these areas, and know that your deliverance is near. The **Points of Deliverance** below do not represent a single act or encounter; each is a *point of reference* that served as a catalyst or turning point.

Emotional Rejection

- Triggers during **Engagement**
  - Fear of rejection and abandonment because of relationship with my Dad. I constantly warred internally, fighting against the fear of my husband, Anthony, unexpectedly leaving me–without any explanation or warning.
  - **Point of Deliverance**: Healing and reconciliation with my natural father. Humility before God and forgiveness.
- Triggers in **Marriage**
  - Feelings of abandonment every time my husband left the room or went to bed early without me on our honeymoon; emotional crisis of abandonment when we became separated on our tenth anniversary cruise.
  - **Point of Deliverance**: The Word of God! Memorizing Psalm 27:10: "When my father and my mother forsake me, then the Lord will take me up" (NIV). Studying The Book of John. Holding on to the promise of Heb. 13:5: "Never will I leave you; never will I forsake you" (NIV).

- Triggers in **Ministry**
  o Writing and speaking rejection letters caused a five- to six-year stoppage in writing for God.
  o **Point of Deliverance**: 2002 Writers' Conference session entitled, "God Speaks." Published an online article in the *Spirit-Led Writer Magazine*. Daily reciting Psalm 139.
  o My husband leaving for a three-week business trip led to an emotional meltdown because my security, my protection was leaving.
  o **Point of Deliverance**: The ministry of reconciliation–total deliverance before my ministry debut. Daily declaring Psalm 27 over myself.

Manifestations

The following were some of my manifestations of the spirit of rejection: Emotional collapse, insecurity, competitive jealousy, disobedience, withdrawal, and procrastination. Too often you and I pay attention to these, which are only **symptoms** of a much deeper issue.

Divine Revelation

- What I **do** is not **who** I am.
- I do not have to be perfect. He who began a good work in me will be faithful to complete it until the day of Jesus Christ (paraphrase).
- I overcome the deep root of the spirit of rejection by faith (Eph. 2:8-10, 3:12); by receiving my inheritance in Christ, and believing who I am in Him.
- God will always protect me emotionally and physically.
- The spirit of rejection will come again; however, I will not entertain it nor can it have any place in my life.
- **Who** I am is **not** defined by how other people treat me or by their opinions of me.
- I am accepted unconditionally loved. I am the righteousness of God in Christ Jesus; therefore, I am acceptable to God. God loves me just the way I am! (2 Cor. 5:21)

Prophetic Deliverance

Our Church had a guest worship leader come for a special night of worship. Apparently, he was a well-known, highly gifted former member of Immanuel's. God sent this messenger, yes–a worship leader–to deliver a prophetic proclamation: "**God**

told me to tell someone here tonight that never again will you suffer from the spirit of rejection; *this is the last day*." I felt shock waves throughout my body! That word pierced by heart and the tears began to flow. I heard sounds coming out of me that I was not even aware of; their origin was somewhere deep inside of me. That word was specifically for me, and I received it! It was a Divine encounter and I was never the same from that day onward.

Sanctuary

The following is my personal account of one desert experience. Here is an excerpt from an 2007 article I wrote entitled, *A Chip Off the Old Block*, where I share about my powerful encounter with God in a way that helped me to overcome the spirit of rejection and other obstacles in my interior life.

> Writer's block–all of us have experienced it. For writers, it's an occupational hazard. But what causes writer's block? Many books and articles have been written on the subject. Studies on this topic reveal a plethora of possible reasons for this impenetrable darkness.
>
> **Called to Write**
>
> Ten years ago, I received God's call to write for His glory. Of course, our calling always requires a time of preparation between the call and the fulfillment of the call. Unaware of this at the time, I started doing research, ordering writers' guidelines and back issues of magazines, assembling binders and so on. Finally, I wrote my first query letter. Feeling a sense of accomplishment, I anxiously waited for a response. The

day of reckoning arrived; although the editor was kind and encouraging, it was still a rejection. The pain of rejection was so unbearable; I did not try again for four years.

During those years of preparation, I realized God gave me a gift to cultivate and use for His glory. I started a communications and public speaking business, using my skills as a business writer. When asked to write an article for a small business newsletter (a paying market), I took another step of faith. On assignment, I wrote an article about trade shows entitled "Show and Tell – Making Trade Shows Work for You." The editor liked it and I got paid! Imagine the boost to my confidence!

The fear of rejection stunted my creativity for many years until one day, I recognized that the editor rejected the piece submitted, *not me*! Over the next six years (1997-2003), I went on to write many articles for local newspapers, newsletters, and even the Internet. Allowing God to build my faith and confidence in *who I am in Him*, enabled me to move on in my calling to write for His glory.

Although God [had] blessed my business writing endeavors, I still had not returned to the Christian Writers' market. Meanwhile, God was building the message I needed for the next step in my writing ministry–my book. You see, I had been through some things: a life threatening family illness; a life threatening personal illness; leaving my church after thirteen years of service; moving my business; and a relocation which separated me from a life of familiarity (a necessary transition for spiritual growth and development). All of which had the power to cause gridlock for any writer. Soon I would discover the horrible disease that had infiltrated my heart, mind–and my writing.

Road to Revelation

In 2005, I decided to test the Christian writing waters. Two publishers at my first Christian writers' conference, in 2002, reviewed the introduction and first two chapters of my book. They offered suggestions, and encouraged me to finish the project.

Armed with positive reinforcement, I revisited the project. After three false starts, I felt too paralyzed to focus. Extremely frustrated, I felt like others were passing me by. Every time I saw a successful author with a best-selling book, discouragement

The Making of a Way Maker

set in and my project did not seem worth pursuing anymore. I could not shake the compulsion to write this book, yet writing it was becoming more and more difficult and I did not understand why. Nevertheless, God was faithful and did not leave me in the dark for long.

He especially used our relocation to Maryland, in 2004, as a catalyst to help me regain my confidence and creativity. I spent time in special communion with God the first two and a half months after our arrival. I sought Him with my whole heart in prayer: "Search me, O God, and know my heart; test me and know my anxious thoughts. See if there is any offensive way in me, and lead me in the way everlasting" (Ps. 139:23-24, NIV). I would later refer to this [period as my time in a place called "Sanctuary." It was a place of transformation.]

Seeking answers, I picked up "The Writer's Workshop in a Box." I began reading the little book inside entitled, "The Art of Writing," edited by Sandra Bark. The chapter on writer's block left me completely devastated! I could not believe what I saw about myself!

Workshop #3, "Understanding and Overcoming Writer's Block," penned by Julia Cameron, also hit home. She noted, "Competition lies at the root of much creative blockage [...] The spirit of competition–as opposed to the spirit of creation–often urges us to quickly winnow out whatever doesn't seem like a winning idea [....]." Talk about hitting the nail on the head!

If these materials were not enough, God led me to another resource: "Exposing the Spirit of Competitive Jealousy," by Creflo A. Dollar, Jr. So, there it was; the deadly disease that blocked my creativity for more than two years: jealous competition. Facing the truth was ugly, painful, and hard to accept. Despite my horror, God was answering my prayer for deliverance.

The enemies of my soul like procrastination, jealous competition, and selfish ambition, threatened my creativity. It was ugly, painful, and hard to accept. Despite my horror, God was answering my prayer. My deliverance started by acknowledging my sin, confession and, finally, repentance. I was rewarded with God's forgiveness and cleansing, and a renewed desire to serve Him with obedience in my writing.

Years later, at the 2005 Christian writer's conference, as I sat in the morning session, I realized I was in a different place than before. Intimacy with God birthed a calm, peaceful assurance of who I am in Christ, a *confidence in His love for me* and what He called me to do. My passion was re-ignited, and I had a renewed commitment to my writing. Obedience yields blessing *and* success!

What is blocking our creativity? What is keeping us from answering the call of God on our lives? No matter how painful, you and I should use these tools to *chip away* at whatever is blocking our breakthrough to restoration. We need to pray, asking God to reveal what may be hindering our faith and creativity. We must humble ourselves, acknowledge and readily confess our sins, asking for and readily receiving His forgiveness. We need to cultivate an intimate relationship with THE source of all creativity! Trust Him. "He who has begun a good work in you, will carry it on to completion until the day of Jesus Christ" (Phil. 1:6).

Benefits and Blessings of Being an Agent of Reconciliation

We can clearly see how critical inner healing is to our success and effectiveness in ministry. Here are even more reasons why we need to enter a time of repentance and cleansing before God can use us:

- To cultivate and maintain healthy relationships–both in the general Body of Christ and in our ministry.
- To have an effective witness; we do not want to bring reproach upon the Gospel of Jesus Christ, due to our poor words or deeds.
- To be effective *Ambassadors for Christ*; we are called to the Kingdom for such a time as this–the last days–to prepare The Way of the Lord for His return.
- To be leaders with influence in the realm of the spirit. When we lead with Kingdom influence, we are able to impact and equip the saints for the work of their ministries.
- To eradicate burnout. Many of us suffer from burnout due to the character defect discussed earlier: **co-dependency**. This emotional malady is quite prevalent in the Body of Christ and one symptom that threatens our

ministry is the inability to serve within and respect healthy **boundaries**.
- To "...be able to withstand in the evil day..." (Eph. 6:13). Our religious freedom is under constant attack and the moral fiber of our country lies in shreds, adding continuous pressure and presenting new challenges for those of us on the front lines. Still, we must be able to stand and endure to the end.
- To be able to maintain our physical health.
- To, most importantly, not cause emotional or spiritual pain to those whom we are called to serve and disciple.

Prayer and intercession: both are essential assets for our spiritual growth as well as the ministry of reconciliation. To pray effectively and prophetically over others, as God leads, we need His discernment, wisdom, and guidance during the time of preparation (Isa. 50:4-5). Prayer and intercession also increase our sensitivity and compassion for others. Compassion for others is born out of seasons of suffering.

As you and I continue to seek God to prepare our hearts for the ministry of reconciliation, we need to be proactive and take the offensive. His yoke is easy and His burden is light. If we walk in the Spirit, we will not fulfill the lusts of the flesh. We do not always have to enter into hand-to-hand combat. As we submit to God the devil **must** flee.

How does God prepare us, His vessels, for service in a way that we do not hurt or wound others out of our own hurts or prejudices?

One way is through the healing power of forgiveness.

The Healing Power of Forgiveness

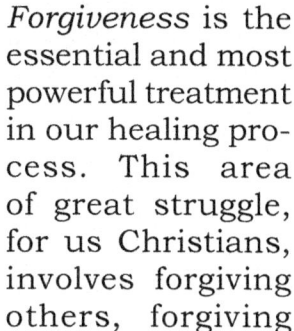

Forgiveness is the essential and most powerful treatment in our healing process.

Forgiveness is the essential and most powerful treatment in our healing process. This area of great struggle, for us Christians, involves forgiving others, forgiving God, and truly forgiving ourselves. There is so much to say on this subject, for it continues to be the single, biggest obstacle and hindrance to spiritual growth in the Body of Christ. Quite frankly, if we cannot overcome this hurdle, then appropriating the principles and abundant life God has ordained for us, as Way Makers, will prove difficult–if not impossible.

Myths Concerning Forgiveness

- The only time we should recall an offense is for the purpose of edification. We present the past offense with the love of Christ for the purpose of growth and maturity in Him. (Isa. 42:3, Matt. 12:20, 2 Cor. 2:7)
- How often should we forgive a repeat offender? The scriptures say if our brother or sister offends us again and

again, we are to forgive him or her "seventy times seven" (Matt. 18:22). In other words, as often as it takes. Should we then constantly put ourselves in harm's way? No. We must learn how to cultivate healthy relationships with **boundaries**. We maintain love, honesty, and respect in all levels of **relationships** (Eph. 5:22-33, 1 Timothy 5).
- Physical, verbal, and emotional abuse should be avoided at all costs. The scriptures say, "If it be possible, as much as lies in you, live peaceably with all men" (Romans 12:18). In some cases, that means removing ourselves from a hostile situation. We are never required to intentionally put ourselves in harm's way.

Dangers and Consequences of Unforgiveness

- Hindrances to our prayers.
- If we do not forgive our brother or sister, our heavenly Father will not forgive us.
- Our spiritual growth is stunted.
- Our spiritual walk is ineffective.
- Our relationships are strained and unprofitable.
- Our witness to others is ineffective.

In our prayer time with God, we have to allow the Holy Spirit to speak to us concerning matters of our heart. We must be open, sharing our heart with Him and allowing Him to give insight, comfort, guidance, direction, and closure. Every day, we should cast our cares upon the Lord because He cares for and watches over us. He will perfect those things that concern us. The earnest prayers of repentance found in Psalms 51 and 139 will lead you into His presence.

Humility and the ability to forgive and ask forgiveness play a major role in our deliverance. When we hurt people – and they, in turn, hurt us – God is not the author of either. He is never responsible for the sins of fallen humanity. I know this to be true in my own life. It was forgiveness that restored an important relationship and *prepared the way for God* to give me the desire of my heart.

"Something Old Turns Into Something New"

A Testimony of Forgiveness and Healing

The music was playing softly in the sanctuary, "There's a ribbon in the sky for our love, do-do-do-da-do-do." I dreamed of walking down the isle to that melody on my wedding day. That day was here. "You okay? Are you ready?" my father asked. "No," I said. "I'm nervous. I hope everything is okay!" "Don't worry. Everything will be fine. I'll be right back." His strong voice was reassuring and comforting. After all, this was a very special day in more ways than one.

I never thought this would be happening for me. It was dream that I thought would never come true. You see I used to hate my father. He married someone else instead of my mother, and had another daughter who would spend her whole life with him; while I was left alone. I felt cheated out of having a father: she had what I always wanted. But mostly, I hated him for not calling or visiting me–not so much as a birthday card for over 20 years!

Reliving some of those painful memories, I remembered being a senior in high school, when my father, a police officer, had been seriously hurt in the line of duty. The doctors didn't think he would make it. My uncle tried to convince me to visit him, telling me that I would regret it later, especially if he didn't survive. But I was so angry I refused to go. With a defiant "no," I hung up the phone.

After graduation, I learned that my father had survived. Some years passed, and surprisingly, my mother and father were talking again! After a few visits, they were actually considering getting back together! But something just wasn't right. He was invited over for the holidays, but he never came. Not then, and not ever again! The reunion never materialized. My anger burned toward him for letting us down yet again!

Ten years passed and in 1986, I received the Lord Jesus Christ as my personal savior. Hungry for the Word of God, I grew strong in my relationship with the Lord. One evening,

"Something Old Turns Into Something New"

the message on forgiveness brought strong conviction about my relationship with my father. Dating someone in a serious relationship, I knew if I wanted a healthy marriage, I had to be reconciled with my father. That night, I was restless and unable to sleep. I didn't know what to do or what to expect. I prayed, "God, I need you to make this reconciliation happen."

The police barracks was noisy: people coming in and out, standing in line, explaining their situations. As I waited for my girlfriend, the Spirit of God spoke to me. "Ask that officer to help you find a police officer." I broke out in a cold sweat. I had to make a choice: be obedient or rationalize my way out of it. Realizing that God was answering my prayer, I chose to be obedient–a decision that would change my life from that point on.

As the officer walked across the room, I said, "Excuse me, officer. I want to find a police officer, but all I have is his name. Could you help me find him?" "Why are you looking for this officer?" he asked. "Because he is my father, I haven't seen him for 20 years and I want to talk to him. Will you help me?" That was all it took. Three officers stopped what they were doing to help me find my father!

The database had too many officers with the same name. The officer asked, "Do you know your father's birthday?" I didn't, but I called someone who should: my mother.

"Mom, I'm at the Police Barracks trying to find my dad. Do you remember his birthday?" She was uncooperative at first, but she finally said, "I think it was March 7th or 8th." I knew he was two years older than her–that told me the year. With that information, they were able to find him. But he had retired from the force some years ago! I thought, now what!

But it was as if God had given these officers a passion for reuniting me with my father! I sat there feelings of excitement and dread at the same time when the officer burst into the room and said, "I'm going to let you talk to your father in a few minutes!" I thought, "How in the world is he going to do that?" Apparently they found my dad's cell phone number. As they dialed, I thought, "What am I going to say?" I pleaded, "God, it's too soon! I'm not prepared to talk to him yet!" The officer's expression changed–the number was no longer in service.

"Whew!!" I said to myself. But, all was not lost. The officers were able to obtain my father's current address. After diligently searching for over an hour on my behalf, they gave me the address and wished me much success.

It's hard to explain how I felt as I left there that day. God had done an amazing thing! It was nothing short of a miracle! But that was only the beginning. I had learned that when making plans, it's wise to seek

"Something Old Turns Into Something New"

godly advice. (Prov. 20:18a) So I decided to seek advice from my Pastor before going any further. His wise and understanding counsel was the foundation for building a new relationship with my father. My first step was to write a letter. "Dear Dad..."

I poured out my heart to him, confessing my judgmental attitude; my error in blaming him; and admitting that having made my own mistakes, I now understood how he could too. I asked him to forgive me for not coming to the hospital, for saying hurtful things to him and about him, and for being mean when he came to visit. Four pages later, God's healing power began to permeate my soul and spirit. I included my address and phone number, and waited. When a card arrived with his phone number inside, it said, **"I forgive you."** *He forgave me!* With tears streaming down my face, I dialed the number.

That was the beginning of a fresh, new life for me! Now, I had a father. A father who loved me and wanted to be with me! Before then, I never realized how deep the void was in my life, until it was filled. I felt wholeness and a sense of security that I never knew before. My father's

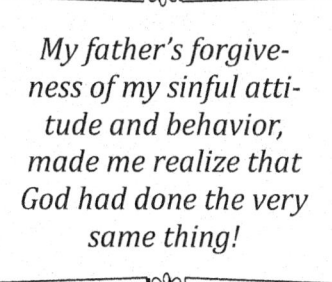

My father's forgiveness of my sinful attitude and behavior, made me realize that God had done the very same thing!

forgiveness of my sinful attitude and behavior, made me realize that God had done the very same thing! I saw God's guidance in the reconciliation process.

I finally saw my father face to face; he looked the same as I remembered…just a little gray. Tears moistened my face as we embraced for a long time. We settled on the sofa and talked for a long time. It was so nice calling him "Dad." When I got engaged, I took my fiancé to meet him, and they became fast friends. My Dad even came to church with us several times. But, my big day was fast approaching. There was just one thing I needed to make my wedding day perfect!

"Dad, I know that we are starting a new relationship, but I was wondering if you would give me away." For a brief moment, I was horrified at the idea that he might say "no." "Are you sure that's what you want?" he asked. "I'm sure. I can't imagine having anyone else but you." "Okay…sure I'll be glad to give you away." I was filled with joy and

> *Because I made the choice to forgive, I experienced the blessings of obedience: unhindered prayer, forgiveness for my sins, joy, peace, and especially, healing in my relationship with my father.*

"Something Old Turns Into Something New"

gratitude to God! Now my wedding day was complete!

What's taking him so long? I was feeling anxious because the enemy tried to tell me that my father was not going to show up. Right at that moment...in walked my Dad. "Are you ready, Sugar?" I breathed a sigh of relief and inwardly kicked the devil in the face! "I think so. Is everybody out there? Is Tony out there?" "Yes, Tony's out there and he is waiting for *you*." He kissed me on the cheek and said, "Let's go." With that, he pulled my veil over my face, and as the music played softly in the air, my father walked me down the aisle. **It was God who had done this thing, and it was marvelous in my eyes!** (Psalm 118:23)

Because I made the choice to forgive, I experienced the blessings of obedience: unhindered prayer, forgiveness for my sins, joy, peace, and especially, healing in my relationship with my father. (Matt. 6:12, 14-15)

Forgiveness is our only road to peace.

Forgiveness is our only road to peace. As we pray this prayer together, we can expect receive God's peace.

A Prayer for Forgiveness

Heavenly Father, You have made it clear that You desire the healing and freedom that forgiveness brings. You said to forgive so that I may be forgiven. By the act of my will, I forgive all who have hurt me out of their own hurts. I release them from any debt and I hold nothing against them. I bless them and release them into your hands.

Father, because Jesus died for me, and His blood was shed for the remission of my sins, I come asking for Your forgiveness for the hurt I have caused others, You, and myself. I confess every thought, word, and deed that was not pleasing in your sight and ask You to cleanse me of all unrighteousness for Your Name's sake. Create in me a clean heart and renew a right spirit within me. I am thankful that because I have confessed my sin, You are faithful and just to forgive and cleanse me. Thank You for healing me on the inside and for restoring the joy of my salvation!

Because You have forgiven me, I choose to forgive myself for all the ways in which I have brought hurt or harm to others and myself. Spirit of the Living God, please forgive me for the times I have grieved You with my poor choices. I forgive myself for the mistakes, accusations, and judgments I have made against myself. I have fallen short of the mark, but Your precious gift to me is eternal life through Jesus Christ. Thank You

"Something Old Turns Into Something New"

for not leaving me dead in my trespasses and sins. You forgive all my iniquities and heal all my diseases (physical, emotional, and spiritual). Thank You that the good work You have begun in me; You are faithful to complete it until the day of Jesus Christ. In Jesus' name I pray, Amen!

The Call of the Way Maker

*"I will send my messenger, who will prepare the way before me. Then suddenly the Lord you are seeking will come to his temple; the messenger of the covenant, whom you desire, will come," says the L*ORD *Almighty."*
Malachi 3:1 NIV

John the Baptist was divinely appointed, by Almighty God, to serve as the *forerunner* of Jesus Christ. Isa. prophesied that he would come to prepare The Way for the Son of God (Isa. 40:3-5). In John 1:23-24, 29-34, the disciple John affirms John the Baptist's calling and the One who sent him. As Way Makers, you and I are also given the mantel–as the one, unified voice of the Body of Christ–to prepare The Way for our returning King. It is a divine commission and calling, one that comes costs a very high price.

Christians are commanded to share the Gospel and make disciples; harmoniously, there is a special calling and anointing for those called to be *forerunners*. First of all, by definition, "***fore***-runners" must go first; they are always up front, ahead of the masses. It takes faith and courage to step out in front. Second, they face tremendous persecution. Everyone thought John the Baptist was a crazy lunatic. And finally, forerunners face extreme opposition and peril, both emotionally and physically. John the Baptist's last

The Way Makers

days on earth were spent in jail and he was devastated that no one came to his rescue. He began to question his call and his mission–probably his very life!

Even though, in the end, he was beheaded, his life and calling were certainly not forgotten nor were they diminished in significance. After all, he was the *forerunner* for the Son of God! Jesus said, "...Among them that are born of women there has not risen one greater than John the Baptist..." (Matt. 11:11, Luke 7:28) The truth is John the Baptist fulfilled his calling in God and went home to be with Father. For him, to live was Christ, and to die was his glorious gain! Amen!

We did not choose Him; but He chose and appointed us so that we might go and bear fruit (John 15:16, NIV). We want to lovingly lead the masses to repentance and salvation. Since we are *Ambassadors for Christ*, He makes His appeal through **us**. We beseech the lost on Christ's behalf: "Be reconciled to God!" Jesus said, "And I, if I be lifted up from the earth, will draw all men unto me" (John 12:32). As Way Makers, we **prepare the way** for Him. At His appearing, He will finish the work.

Jesus was John the Baptist's whole life: He was the sole reason for his birth! He did not have a *normal* life, according to the standards of the day. He was separated from society; living and preaching out in the desert. He was set apart for a specific purpose – noble purpose–and he fulfilled it without wavering or distraction. In the same way, we must accept that our lives are not our own; we have also been bought with a price.

Way Makers are divinely chosen before the foundation of the world. We were hand-picked to usher in our returning King, Jesus Christ. We have already been ordained for this special assignment (Eph. 2:10). Our calling is irrevocable and without repentance: God will not change His mind. We make our calling and election sure by walking worthy of the vocation to which we are called. (2 Pet. 1:10)

The Fear of the Lord

"The fear of the Lord is the beginning of wisdom..." (Psalm 111:10, Proverbs 1:7, 9:10). In 2 Cor. 5:11 (NIV), Paul states, "Since, then, we know what it is to fear the Lord, we try to persuade others. What we are is plain to God, and I hope it is also plain to your conscience." Earlier in this chapter, he talks about the deeds done in the body–whether good or bad–and how we will all stand before God to give an account. This is why it is so important that we **serve to please God and not man**.

We know what it means to experience the awesome power of God in such a way that it inspires awe and reverence for who God is. After all, the disciples were eyewitnesses to Jesus' death, burial, and glorious resurrection.

Try to imagine the reverential fear of God that permeated their very souls when they encountered Jesus after His resurrection! It is something so phenomenal that it births an extreme reverence for the only power completely superior to anything we have ever known. The message that won the First Century Church was, *Jesus died and rose again! He is alive!* The resurrection power of Jesus Christ demands our utmost respect and reverence.

The Call of the Way Maker

Paul is another perfect example of one who walked out his calling with reverential fear of the Lord, after his life-altering encounter with Jesus on the road to Damascus! Despite opposition, fear, distrust from the Church and religious leaders, after his conversion, Paul fearlessly declared *who* and *whose* he was, and he preached The Gospel with boldness.

However, the Corinthian Church was not willing to accept his counsel. In fact, they questioned his right to say anything to them at all! They questioned his leadership and authority, approaching him from a worldly point of view by asking him for credentials: a letter of recommendation, leading to his response in 2 Cor. 3:1-6.

> "Do we begin again to commend ourselves or need we, as some others, epistles of commendation to you, or letters of commendation from you? Ye are our epistle written in our hearts, known and read of all men: Forasmuch as ye are manifestly declared to be the epistle of Christ ministered by us, written not with ink, but with the Spirit of the living God; not in tables of stone, but in fleshy tables of the heart, and such trust have we through Christ to God-ward:
> Not that we are sufficient of ourselves to think anything as of ourselves;

The Way Makers

but our sufficiency is of God who also has made us able ministers of the New Testament–not of the letter, but of the spirit: for the letter kills, but the spirit gives life."

Paul lets them know that it is **God** who made him a competent minister of The Gospel. Indeed, we need to acknowledge that ***it is God who equips us***. God makes us competent; evidenced by our ministry to those He gives us by His Spirit: *the Believers in Corinth were Paul's letter of recommendation!*

Those God gives us could care less about our intellectual knowledge. They want to know that we ***care*** (2 Cor. 6:11-13). In his letter to the church in Philippi, Paul says if anybody had reason to boast about heritage, lineage, and education, he had more reasons than anybody. "...I count all things but loss for the excellency of the knowledge of Christ Jesus my Lord..." (Phil. 3:1-11). Yes, we must be knowledgeable, but not by human standards only.

Yes, we must be knowledgeable, but not by human standards only.

Now, of course, I am not saying that learning and preparation are not important; we must meet the requirements to complete our education. In spite of those requirements, we are not to lose sight of the fact that knowledge without the Spirit of God puffs us up and leads only to our spiritual death – and the death of our ministry.

Answering the Call – A Personal Testimony

I remember when God called me like it was yesterday...

I recently shared my testimony of when I received and acknowledged the call of God on my life as well as my response to His call. I would like to share that experience because, as I reflect, I find it important to recognize who God used to make this divine declaration: the prophet Jeremiah. In Jeremiah, Chapter 1, when God called Jeremiah, He also called me. Although I did not make the connection at that time, I later discovered that Jeremiah and I have a lot in common. God called him to deliver His message to the people of Israel, but Jeremiah was afraid of what they would think. He did not believe they would listen to Him because of His age. He was also intimidated by their faces – their response (Jer. 1:7-8). Well that ***was*** me! I say that because though I am not where I want to be, I am thankfully not where I used to be either! Praise The Lord!

When I said, "Yes" to God, from that moment up to the present, I fought against fierce opposition. The devil even used Christians – my superiors, those in spiritual authority over me, and so-called friends to squelch the Word of the Lord in my mouth!

The Call of the Way Maker

So many examples come flooding back to me as I reflect on my journey. I remember so many times opening my mouth to share, only to be shut down, disregarded, and even discredited. Still, God would send confirmation of what He said to me, so I would not be discouraged or tempted to quit. So many times, I was left hurting, wondering if I really did have anything Kingdom-worthy to say. The most recent instance occurred when I announced that I was stepping down from a leadership role in to focus on this book. An overseeing pastor of the ministry said to me, "So, what are you going to write about that we have not heard already?" How is that for a word of encouragement? I admit it stung; yet, it did not stop me!

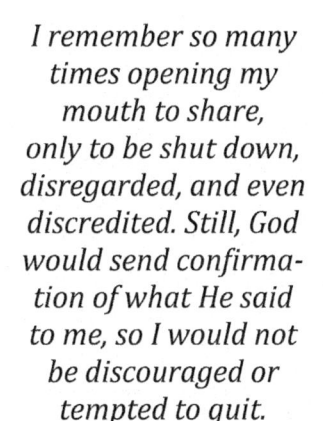

> *I remember so many times opening my mouth to share, only to be shut down, disregarded, and even discredited. Still, God would send confirmation of what He said to me, so I would not be discouraged or tempted to quit.*

I asked God, "Why so much opposition?" He impressed upon my heart Matt. 11:12: "And from the days of John the Baptist until now the kingdom of heaven suffers violence, and the violent take it by force." This word became bread for me. My Kingdom assignment will suffer persecution. The work of faith is to believe; to overcome and to persevere. It comes with the territory. A great and effectual door is open unto me; yet, there are many adversaries – much opposition – that threaten to hinder or stop my progress! (1 Cor. 16:9) The weapons of my warfare are not carnal (worldly or fleshly); they are mighty through God. I have at my disposal an arsenal that will utterly destroy the enemy of my soul (2 Cor. 10:3-5). The opposition continues to this day; however, in the words of the late Maya Angelou, **"*Still I Rise!*"**[2]. Like the prophet Jeremiah, I am no longer looking at the intimidating faces of those who need to hear my God-given message!

So, I make declaration today: My name is Angela M. Gracey, Apostolic Messenger of God, *Ambassador of Christ*, and a Way Maker; a Teacher and Leader. I use my God-given gifts to declare His message of reconciliation. I have been called to raise up Way Makers – including ***you*** – all over the world to prepare **The Way** for our returning King, Jesus Christ!

Today, God has called ***you and me*** to be Way Makers! We have what it takes to overcome. Every day, we put on the whole armor of God, take up our weapons and fight the good fight of faith! Greater is He that is in us than he that is in the world! (1 John 4:4) We have world-overcoming faith inside of us! And since God is for us, the devil and all of hell cannot stand against us! We have His Word on it! (Romans 8:31)

Dead to "Self" Life

Living the Exchanged Life

Holy living is absolutely essential for a Way Maker. God commands us to "'... [be] holy because I, the Lord your God, am holy'" (Lev. 19:2). What does that mean in respect to our lives as Way Makers? What attitude or mindset must we demonstrate in our walk?

It starts with us having a healthy and reverential fear of the Lord. "The fear of the Lord is the beginning of wisdom and knowledge of the Holy One is understanding." (Prov. 9:10) Recognizing the sovereign, omnipotent God as the Lord over all creation – yet the personal God of our salvation – should forever dictate how we live our lives daily in relation to God and others.

Next, we have to recognize that we are **called**. God's gifts and calling are irrevocable and without repentance. God will not change His mind (Matt. 5:13, 2 Pet. 1:10). There are certain characteristics present in those of us called to be Way Makers:

- Commitment
- Faithfulness
- Humility
- Trustworthy
- Obedience

To be crucified with Christ (meaning, we entered into His death through the waters of baptism), is to surrender our "self" life and give Christ absolute freedom to live in and through us. *"I have been crucified with Christ and I no longer live, but Christ lives in me. The life I now live in the body, I live by faith in the Son of God, who loved me and gave himself for me"* (Gal. 2:20). This is the **exchanged** life.

Jesus said, "If any man will come after me, let him deny himself, and take up his cross, and follow me." (Matt. 16:24, Mark 8:34, Luke 9:23). That means to die to what we want and fully submit to what God wants. This is a painful process in the growth and development of all Christian leaders. In our society of instant gratification, we want our desires addressed right now! We do not want to be denied. However, as true disciples – taught of the Lord – we must be humble, teachable servants. We die daily to our sinful nature. We can no longer live unto to ourselves; we live for Jesus Christ who died for us. Jesus also said, "...[except] a corn of wheat falls into the ground and dies, it abides alone: but if it dies, it brings forth much fruit" (John 12:24).

"And he died for all, that those who live should no longer live for themselves but for him who died for them and was raised again." (2 Cor. 5:15) What does this mean? The cross is the cross of suffering. It is the symbol of the enormous burden of sin He bore for all of mankind. We, too, are called to suffer for Christ's sake. Jesus said, in this life we will face persecution; there will be testing, trials, and opposition. Our lives are not our own. We have been bought with a price. If we want to partake in Jesus Christ's glory, we must also share in His suffering. Paul describes it as, "...the fellowship of His sufferings..." (Phil. 3:10) In 2 Cor. 4:8-10, Paul describes suffering this way: "We are hard pressed on every side, but not crushed; perplexed, but not in despair; persecuted, but not abandoned; struck down, but not destroyed. We always carry around in our body the death of Jesus, so that the life of Jesus may also be revealed in our body."

Earlier, we talked about what it means to endure. We are blessed when we endure hardship for Christ's sake. In fact, scripture tells us we should count it a privilege. Just remember, no sacrifice will go unrewarded. Your labor in the Lord is **never** in vain!

7 Callings of the Way Maker

Way Makers are called to:

1. **Come out from among the world and be separate** (sanctified; set apart) for Kingdom purposes. (Rom. 12:1-2)
2. **Sanctification**. Sanctify yourselves; you're about to cross over to the other side. (Joshua 3)
3. **Be ready**. The Bride of Christ must make herself ready. Jesus is coming back for a church without spot nor wrinkle! (Eph. 5:26-27)
4. **Pray**. If God's people would humble themselves and intercede, He will hear from heaven, forgive our sins, and heal our land. (2 Chron. 7:14)
5. **Co-labor with Him**. The harvest is plentiful, but the laborers are few. God is calling His co-laborers into the vineyard. (Luke 10:2)
6. **Prepare the Way of The Lord**, as Ambassadors of Christ, fulfilling the Great Commission through the ministry and message of reconciliation. (Matt. 28:18; 2 Cor. 5:11-6:2)
7. **Usher in the return of our Lord and Savior**, Jesus Christ. Sound the alarm: "The Bridegroom is coming!" He will make the *final call* when He calls us to meet Him together in the

air; and so shall we ever be with the Lord! (Matt. 25; 1 Thess. 4:15-17)

Can you articulate what God has called you to do in this end-time hour? Is there anything distracting you from God or keeping you from making progress in the Lord? What do you need to do in order to focus more fully on the call of God on your life? Are you on God's agenda or your agenda? Can you identify any emotional hindrances that keep you from embracing your destiny?

The Characteristics of a Way Maker

The next day John saw Jesus coming toward him and said, "Look, the Lamb of God, who takes away the sin of the world! This is the one I meant when I said, 'A man who comes after me has surpassed me because he was before me.' I myself did not know him, but the reason I came baptizing with water was that he might be revealed to Israel." Then John gave this testimony: "I saw the Spirit come down from heaven as a dove and remain on him. And I myself did not know him, but the one who sent me to baptize with water told me, 'The man on whom you see the Spirit come down and remain is the one who will baptize with the Holy Spirit.' I have seen and I testify that this is God's Chosen One." The next day John was there again with two of his disciples. When he saw Jesus passing by, he said, "Look, the Lamb of God!" When the two disciples heard him say this, they followed Jesus. Turning around, Jesus saw them following and asked, "What do you want?" They said, "Rabbi" (which means "Teacher"), "where are you staying?" "Come," he replied, "and you will see." So they went and saw where he was staying, and they spent that day with him. It was about four in the afternoon. Andrew, Simon Peter's brother, was one of the two who heard what John had said and who had followed Jesus. The first thing Andrew did was to find his brother Simon and tell him, "We have found the Messiah" (that is, the Christ). And he brought him to Jesus. John 1:29-42 NIV

An argument developed between some of John's disciples and a certain Jew over the matter of ceremonial washing.
They came to John and said to him, "Rabbi, that man who was with you on the other side of the Jordan—the one you testified about—look, he is baptizing, and everyone is going to him."

To this John replied, "A person can receive only what is given them from heaven. You yourselves can testify that I said, 'I am not the Messiah but am sent ahead of him.' The bride belongs to the bridegroom. The friend who attends the bridegroom waits and listens for him, and is full of joy when he hears the bridegroom's voice. That joy is mine, and it is now complete. He must become greater; I must become less." John 3:25-30 NIV

The Characteristics of a Way Maker

In this prophetic hour, Way Makers must accurately see and hear God, and only do what we see the Father doing. He will tell us what to say and what to do. This prophetic hour also requires our **absolute obedience** to God. I'm not suggesting perfection, but a willingness to seek Him with our whole hearts and then to obey. John the Baptist continues to be our example of a Godly Way Maker: one who literally prepared ***the way*** of the Lord (John 1:19-42; 3:25-36). Here are some of the characteristics revealed in John the Baptist as an example for Way Makers today:

- ***Way Makers do not claim anything that rightfully belongs to God***. We do not think more highly of themselves than we ought. John the Baptist "did not fail to confess, but confessed freely, 'I am not the Christ'" (John 1:20).

- **Way Makers are humble and do not seek a glamorous reputation (or fame).** John the Baptist identified himself by the prophecy spoken about him (Matt. 3:11, John 1:21-23, 26-27).
- **Way Makers know their roles and their purpose.** We only function in our calling; in other words, we stay in our lane. John the Baptist clearly articulated who he was and his purpose–in relationship to Jesus. He was on one side of the Jordan while Jesus was on the other; he stayed on his side of the river (John 1:24-28).
- **Way Makers always point to Jesus and His deity.** Every spirit that does not acknowledge Jesus in the flesh is not of God. John the Baptist did not really know or understand everything about Jesus, but he knew the reason He came to him to be baptized in water, was so that Jesus would be revealed. John the Baptist was obedient even though he did not understand everything. Then, he testifies about his own spiritual revelation. He would not have known except that *"the one who sent me...told me,"* by revelation of the Holy Spirit that Jesus was, indeed, the Son of God (John 1:29-39, 3:22-36).

- ***Way Makers always point and guide others to Jesus because of the anointing on their message***. Did John the Baptist complete the work the Father gave him to do? Absolutely! Jesus' followers were first disciples of John the Baptist; he prepared their hearts for the call. Just as Jesus, by the Holy Spirit, prepares us for our calling. When it was time to respond to their call, they immediately dropped everything and followed Him (John 1:35-42).
- ***Way Makers make disciples***. Interesting note: the first thing Jesus did when He began His ministry was choose twelve disciples. Should we not do the same? The scripture admonishes us that what we have learned, the same commit to faithful men and women. Therefore, I am on a mission to pour into at least 12 leaders. I'm looking for a team of Ambassadors to join me on this assignment. (See contact information at the end of the book.) (John 1:35-42)
- ***Way Makers confront hypocrisy and deception, exercising their divinely delegated authority***. They speak The Truth with power. John the Baptist boldly confronted the hypocrisy of the Sanhedrin and exposed their deception. The scriptures say in

The Characteristics of a Way Maker

the last days, the people of the world will call right wrong and wrong right. They will refuse to accept anything that is absolute truth. Today, truth is already considered relative (Matt. 3:7-10).

- ***Way Makers are dead to selfish ambitions and worldly plans***. We cannot prepare the Way for Jesus Christ's return unless we have completely surrendered our lives to Him. *We must decrease and He must increase.* Our lives should be so hidden in Christ that not flesh is glorified in His sight. It is the life of Christ that must be seen in us; nothing else will please the Father. Only what we do for Christ will last (John 3:25-36).

These characteristics must be evident in our lives in some measure in order for us to carry out our role as Way Makers. Although we will make mistakes, God's grace is sufficient. The most important thing is that our hearts are committed to obeying Him.

Do you recognize any of these characteristics in your own life? What areas present a struggle for you? Ask God to empower you by His Spirit. Examine your own motives. What are you doing to prepare the way of the Lord? Why are you doing it?

The Role of a Way Maker

Now this was John's testimony when the Jewish leaders in Jerusalem sent priests and Levites to ask him who he was. He did not fail to confess, but confessed freely, "I am not the Messiah." They asked him, "Then who are you? Are you Elijah?" He said, "I am not." "Are you the Prophet?" He answered, "No." Finally they said, "Who are you? Give us an answer to take back to those who sent us. What do you say about yourself?" John replied in the words of Isa. the prophet, "I am the voice of one calling in the wilderness, 'Make straight the way for the Lord.'" Now the Pharisees who had been sent questioned him, "Why then do you baptize if you are not the Messiah, nor Elijah, nor the Prophet?" "I baptize with water," John replied, *"but among you stands one you do not know. He is the one who comes after me, the straps of whose sandals I am not worthy to untie."* John 1:19-27 NIV

The Role of a Way Maker

As Way Makers, our role is also our responsibility. God has entrusted us with the ministry and message of reconciliation. God reconciled the world to Himself through Jesus Christ; so, we are now *Ambassadors for Christ.* As ambassadors, we have the same power and authority as the government or kingdom we represent. Jesus said, "...All authority in heaven and on earth has been given to me..." (Matt. 28:18, NIV); and, "...As the Father has sent me, I am sending you..." (John 20:21, NIV). We have that same power and authority, of carrying the mantel and the anointing of John the Baptist, to fulfill the mandate of preparing the Way for Jesus Christ's return.

Spiritual Parenthood

"Even if you had ten thousand guardians in Christ, you do not have many fathers, for in Christ Jesus I became your father

The Role of a Way Maker

through the Gospel. Therefore, I urge you to **imitate me**." (1 Cor. 4:15-6, emphasis added).

As Way Makers, one of our chief responsibilities is to be spiritual parents – like Paul. What I love about Paul: he saw himself as a *father in the faith*. He ministered to the Gentiles as a father would to his children: gentle, yet firm in his instruction. He watched over them, prayed for them, and gave of himself to the point of neglecting his own care! Indeed, he often risked his very life, traveling from one congregation to another.

In these last days, you and I need to be men and women, who are committed to making disciples as well as being spiritual fathers and mothers (spiritual parents) in the faith. It is time we stop looking only at our personal interests, and reach out to care for others. There are many gifts in the Body of Christ; still, these gifts need sound guidance and mentoring from healthy

> *In these last days, you and I need to be men and women, who are committed to making disciples as well as being spiritual fathers and mothers (spiritual parents) in the faith. It is time we stop looking only at our personal interests, and reach out to care for others.*

leaders in ministry. Teaching is wonderful; it is one of the five-fold ministry gifts given for the equipping of the saints. However, we need more than just Bible scholars; we need men and women leaders, with loving and compassionate hearts, who can effectively train and mentor new disciples daily entering the Kingdom.

I am sure many of us wish we had spiritual parents or mentors currently speaking into our lives. Or, for some of us, who used to have spiritual parents or mentors at certain times in our lives, we know the real treasure and value of those relationships.

Discipleship

In John 15, we are admonished to bear fruit–fruit that remains. We are not to just pursue converts, but make disciples–future leaders. There are souls God has pre-destined to our specific area(s) of ministry – whether we reach them one-on-one or in a group. The only way we can effectively fulfill our noble calling to be spiritual parents or mentors is to reproduce ourselves in others. We have many examples in the Bible: Moses and Joshua; Elijah and Elisha; Paul for Timothy and Titus; and most importantly, Jesus and His Twelve Disciples.

Our responsibility as spiritual parents or mentors also includes protecting new disciples from error and falsehood as God leads and empowers us. We do this by faithfully holding out the Word of Truth (2 Timothy 3:16-17), as well as ministering to their physical needs. As spiritual parents we are responsible for setting the example and establishing healthy boundaries for spiritual growth.

Peacemakers

"But in your hearts set apart Christ as Lord. Always be prepared to give an answer to everyone who asks you to give the reason for the hope that you have. But do this with **gentleness and respect**..." (1 Pet. 3:15, emphasis added).

Way Makers are **_peacemakers_** – not just _peacekeepers_! As peacemakers, we lay down or forfeit our rights for the sake of reconciliation. Biblical examples of some characteristics found in us, peacemakers, include:

- Not intentionally causing our brothers, sisters, sons, or daughters – biological and spiritual – to stumble in any way, especially by what we eat and drink (Romans 14).
- Learning how to effectively communicate with different types of people. Paul states, "...I have become all things to all people so that by all possible means I might save some..." (1 Cor. 9:19-23)

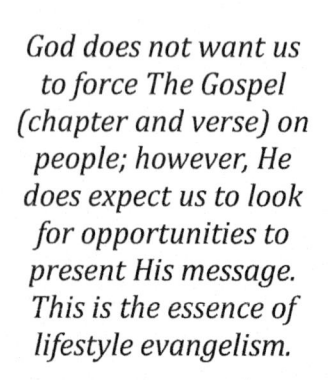

God does not want us to force The Gospel (chapter and verse) on people; however, He does expect us to look for opportunities to present His message. This is the essence of lifestyle evangelism.

God does not want us to force The Gospel (chapter and verse) on people; however, He does expect us to look for opportunities to present His message. This is the essence of lifestyle evangelism.

In order for us to reach this lost, dying world with The Gospel, ministering to the hurting, the bound, and brokenhearted, we must do it within the context of healthy relationships. Through His Word, God gives us practical principles for healthy relationships:

- Love genuinely from the core of our beings; do not fake it (1 Cor. 13).
- Be slow to speak, slow to anger, but plenteous in mercy (Psalm 86:15, 103:8, James 1:19-20).
- Do not hold grudges. Be quick to forgive. Overlook petty offenses (1 Peter 4:8).
- Do not think more highly of ourselves than we ought; esteem others more highly than ourselves (Romans 12:3, Phil. 2:3).
- Run from evil; hold on to the good. Run from gossip, complaining, backbiting, and murmuring (Romans 12:9, Phil. 2:14-16, 1 Thessalonians 5:21-22).
- Be good friends, who love deeply. If you desire friends, you must show

The Way Makers

yourself *friendly* (Proverbs 27:6, Romans 12:9-21).
- Help those in need; be creative in hospitality (1 Tim. 5:16).
- Bless our enemies; do not curse them under our breath (Matt. 5:43-48, Luke 6:27-28, Rom. 12:14).
- Rejoice with those who rejoice; mourn with those who mourn (Romans 12:15).
- Get along with each other; do not be stuck-up. Make friends with nobodies; do not try to be the greatest (Rom. 12:16).
- Do not hit back (Matt. 5:38-42, Luke 6:29).
- As much as lies within us, we are to get along with everyone. (Rom. 12:18).
- Do not insist on getting even; that is not for us to do. "...Do not take revenge, my dear friends, but leave room for God's wrath, for it is written: 'It is mine to avenge; I will repay,' says the Lord." (Rom. 12:19).
- "If [our enemies are] hungry, feed [them]; if [they are] thirsty, give [them] something to drink. In doing this, [we] will heap burning coals on [their heads]" (Rom. 12:20).
- Do not let evil (strife, jealousy, anger, selfish ambition, and pride) get the best of us; get the best of evil by doing good–especially to those in

the household of faith (Gal. 6:10; 1 Thess. 5:15).

As peace-making Way Makers, we are also *lifestyle evangelists*. The following characteristics are critical to our effectiveness in lifestyle evangelism:

- ***Personal Relationship with God*** – Evidence of our on-going fellowship with God.
- ***Personal Witness*** – Our conduct is consistent with our conversation.
- ***Personal Testimony*** – We must be transparent in sharing the reason for our hope!
- ***Personal Commitment to Calling*** – Our faithfulness pleases God and prepares us for our destiny.
- ***Minister to the Lord as priests***. We give ourselves to the Word, praise and worship, prayer, and intercession. We establish an intimate relationship with God and learn to abide in His presence.
- ***Offer sacrifices to the Lord of***:
    - Our bodies, holy and acceptable unto Him.
    - Praise and worship.
    - The first fruits of our increase.
    - Surrendering our lives for the cause of Christ.

- **Discipleship**–After we become disciples we then go and make disciples (Matt. 28:18-20), baptizing them in the name of the Father, the Son, and the Holy Spirit; we guide them as they learn to obey everything He has commanded us to do while on earth (Isa. 50:5-6).
- **Fulfilling the Great Commission**– Being Way Makers (preparing **the Way** of the Lord) involves more than just evangelism and superficial discipleship. As we are molded in the image of Jesus Christ, we then duplicate ourselves by making disciples.
- ***Cultivation of Spiritual and Ministry Gifts***–Make our calling and election sure. In 1 Timothy, Paul admonishes Timothy to "stir up the gift" within him. He instructs Timothy to give himself daily to teaching the Word and to the ministry. We have to practice (make use of) the ministry gifts that were recognized in us by the laying on of hands (Eph. 4). As we mature in Christ and our gifting, our calling and election are made all the more established, allowing us to use them with power and authority through Jesus Christ. If we are lazy, we become ineffective and unproductive in the Kingdom, short-circuiting our vision and destiny.

"Blessed are the peacemakers: for they shall be called the children of God" (Matt. 5:9, emphasis added). I want to challenge us to **endeavor to keep the spirit of unity in the bond of peace**; to be makers and maintainers of peace from this day forward. Peacemakers, who sow in peace, will reap a harvest of righteousness (Matt. 5:6, Eph. 4:3, James 3:18).

What commitment(s) are you prepared to make to be a peacemaker? Are you willing to give up your rights for the cause of peace? Take inventory of your relationships; how healthy are they on a scale from 1 to 10? Are you holding grudges? How can you be more effective in your personal witness?

The Message of a Way Maker

"In those days John the Baptist came, preaching in the wilderness of Judea and saying, "Repent, for the kingdom of heaven has come near." Matt. 3:1-2

The Message and Ministry of Reconciliation

"To wit, that God was in Christ, reconciling the world unto Himself, not imputing their trespasses unto them; and hath committed unto us the word of reconciliation. Now then we are ambassadors for Christ, as though God did beseech you by us: we pray you in Christ's stead, be ye reconciled to God. For he hath made him to be sin for us, who knew no sin; that we might be made the righteousness of God in him. We then, as workers together with him, beseech you also that ye receive not the grace of God in vain. (For he saith, I have heard thee in a time accepted, and in the day of salvation have I succored thee: behold, now is the accepted time; behold, now is the day of salvation." (2 Cor. 5:19-6:2).

The **message** of reconciliation is the message of the Way Maker. The **ministry** of reconciliation is the process or method by which reconciliation takes place. Therefore, the message and ministry of reconciliation are the means to evangelism. There are different types or methods of evangelism and we are going to look at some of them later in this book; one method examined will be, in my opinion, most effective in these end times. For now, let us see **how** the message and ministry of reconciliation are intricately related.

The Ministry of Reconciliation

> "Since, then, we know what it is to fear the Lord, we try to persuade others. What we are is plain to God, and I hope it is also plain to your conscience. We are not trying to commend ourselves to you again, but are giving you an opportunity to take pride in us, so that you can answer those who take pride in what is seen rather than in what is in the heart. If we are "out of our mind," as some say, it is for God; if we are in our right mind, it is for you. For Christ's love compels us, because we are convinced that one died for all, and therefore all died. And he died for all, that those who live should no longer

live for themselves but for him who died for them and was raised again.

So from now on we regard no one from a worldly point of view. Though we once regarded Christ in this way, we do so no longer. Therefore, if anyone is in Christ, the new creation has come: The old has gone, the new is here! All this is from God, who reconciled us to himself through Christ and **gave us the ministry of reconciliation"** (2 Cor. 5:11-18, emphasis added).

Webster's Dictionary defines *reconciliation as*: settlement, understanding, bring into agreement, compromise, reunion, cease-fire, restoration, and resolution.

The ministry of reconciliation, at its core, is the process of conflict resolution. The minister of reconciliation is an *Ambassador for Christ*, first in Jerusalem, then in Samaria, and to the uttermost ends of the earth. As Way Makers, we are ambassadors **commissioned to facilitate conflict resolution**. Conflict arises out of division and separation between two or more entities, including:

- Nation against Nation
- Cultural Conflicts
- Religious Belief Conflicts
- Racial Conflicts
- Generational Conflicts

- Gender Conflicts

The **supreme conflict** is between man and Father God. *Ambassadors for Christ* travel from continent to continent; nation to nation; city to city, resolving this conflict. We must represent Christ–look, talk, and act like Him. He is the focus–we are preparing the Way for His return by resolving the conflict between man and His Father. In this prophetic hour, us Way Makers must accurately see and hear God, only doing what we see the Father doing. He will tell us what to say and do. This prophetic hour also necessitates our **absolute obedience** to God.

> "***Therefore, if anyone is in Christ, he is a new creation; the old has gone, the new has come!***" (2 Cor. 5:17, emphasis added). Hallelujah!

Selah

The Message of Reconciliation

Jesus was baptized and led into the wilderness to be tested of the devil. When He emerged, full of power in the Holy Spirit, He began His public ministry with the same message as John the Baptist: "Repent, and be baptized!" As *Ambassadors for Christ*, we follow His lead as we, too, make that same declaration: "Repent, and be baptized!" (Matt. 4:17, John 3:31-36)

When the Spirit of Truth comes, He will not speak on His own authority, but only what He hears from the Father. The same Spirit of Truth lives in us; we know His voice and the voice of a stranger we will not follow. All authority has been given to us through Jesus Christ; therefore, we speak The Truth to the lies of the enemy on every occasion. There is no question of the power of God's Word. The scriptures declare that "The Gospel is the power of God unto salvation!" We are called and instructed to preach the word in season and out of season. Study to show yourself approved, rightly dividing the Word of Truth. Beware of false doctrine. Warn and protect the brethren. Make our calling and election sure. Declare the Word of the Lord!

The Mission of a Way Maker

"And you, my child, will be called a prophet of the Most High; for you will go on before the Lord to prepare the way for Him, to give His people the knowledge of salvation through the forgiveness of their sins,..."
Luke 1:76-77

The Great Commission

John the Baptist had one mission and one mission only: to prepare the way of the Lord by leading them to a spiritual condition of the heart so that they were ready to receive the baptism of the Holy Spirit through the Lord Jesus Christ.

We have a prophetic calling to edify the lost, to make them knowledgeable about this great salvation. We are His Ambassadors of the Kingdom! God makes His appeal through us: "Be reconciled to God!" (2 Cor. 5:20)

> Then Jesus came to them and said, *"All authority in heaven and on earth has been given to me. Therefore go and make disciples of all nations, baptizing them in the name of the Father and of the Son and of the Holy Spirit, and teaching them to obey everything I have commanded you. And surely I am with you always, to the very end of the age."* (Matt. 28:18-20).

Jesus clearly states our responsibility and destiny to be fulfilled in the earth before His return. Jesus is coming back for The Body of Christ, His unified Bride–without spot or blemish. We want to be found, not having a righteousness of our own, but dressed in His righteousness and presented faultless before His throne with exceeding joy.

Preach the Gospel

These are, indeed, the last days vividly described in the scriptures. Our focus must be not on the day or the hour, or whether the rapture will happen pre- or post-tribulation. We must be steadfast in our faith; enduring to the very end.

Be sober and vigilant as the Day of Judgment approaches. "As long as it is day, we must do the works of him who sent me. Night is coming, when no one can work. While I am in the world, I am the light of the world" (John 9:5-4, NIV). Our primary and supreme goal is to take as many souls with us to Heaven as we can, leading them to the ark of safety. Our message: "Repent! Get into the ark of safety!"

We must also be prepared for a tremendous outpouring of the Holy Spirit. Yes, these are perilous times, but we only need to look up–for our redemption draws near. Arise! Shine! Our light has come! (Isa. 60)

We must **be** Christians, letting our light shine brightly in this dark world.

The message of The Gospel of Jesus Christ is declared in different ways by different people, but endures unchanged. Likewise, the mission may be carried out in different ways, depending on our gifts and talents; yet, it remains the same: fulfill The Great Commission.

And there are different methods or means by which to carry out the mission, including what is commonly referred to as "The Roman Road to Salvation" (Romans 3:10-11, 23, 6:23, 10:9-10).

No matter the means, we declare that Jesus is the Son of God, who takes away the sins of the world! The most important part of our witness and the most powerful strategy we have is the ability to boldly share our faith with others.

Be Ready to Give an Answer

The Sadducees were always **judging by the outward appearance**: ceremonial acts of righteousness that no longer applied under the law of grace. **God looks at the heart**. In 2 Cor. 5:11-12, Paul earnestly says, "Since, then, we know what it is to fear the Lord, we try to persuade others. What we are is plain to God, and I hope it is also plain to your conscience. We are not trying to commend ourselves to you again, but are giving you an opportunity to take pride in us, so that you can answer those who take pride in what is seen rather than in what is in the heart."

Do you know what it means to fear the Lord? Do you know what it is like:

- To be forgiven, delivered, and changed forever?
- To be dead in trespasses and sins and then born again to a new life and peace with God?
- To be called out of darkness into His marvelous light?

Your ability to answer these questions, leads to the development of your personal testimony of what God has done in your life.

Your Testimony

Your testimony is one of your most powerful tools of ministry as a Way Maker. The scriptures say, in Revelation 12:11, "...[We overcome the devil] by the blood of the Lamb, and by the word of [our] testimony..." Every trial and tribulation you experience is for the benefit of your spiritual growth and the spiritual growth of those God leads you to serve in your ministry. The greater the trial or test, the greater the purpose and plans God has for your life.

When you enter into the suffering of the human condition (struggle, illness, loss) you emerge with a spirit of compassion. The by-product of a tried and tested life is your greater capacity to love and show the compassion of Christ. God uses these experiences to build your message – your testimony. Your "mess"

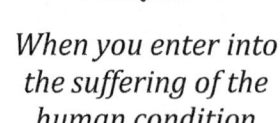

> *When you enter into the suffering of the human condition (struggle, illness, loss) you emerge with a spirit of compassion.*

is transformed into a "message" of encouragement, strengthening others as they invite the Lord to have His in their lives!

You have a testimony! God has done amazing things in your life! He has saved, healed, and delivered you in so many ways.

It is vitally important that you communicate what He has done with holy boldness to the people in this lost and dying world. They need it and are looking for it! They are looking for you–a true *Ambassador for Christ*–to live out the love of God with authenticity and sincerity. Your testimony is vital. The scriptures say you should be *"... prepared to give an answer to everyone who asks you to give the reason for the hope that you have. But do this with gentleness and respect..."* (1 Peter 3:15, emphasis added).

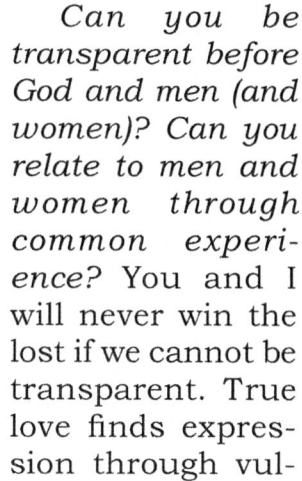

> *"...prepared to give an answer to everyone who asks you to give the reason for the hope that you have. But do this with gentleness and respect..."*

Can you be transparent before God and men (and women)? Can you relate to men and women through common experience? You and I will never win the lost if we cannot be transparent. True love finds expression through vulnerability. We are not able to properly express or feel love if we have not even opened up our own heart to receive the transforming love of God. When others can see, through the message of our testimonies, a glimpse of our lives before and after Christ, then faith and hope arise. If God could save and use us, He can certainly rescue them too.

"The fear of the Lord is the beginning of wisdom and knowledge of the Holy One is understanding" (Prov. 9:10). Unless we are born again of the Spirit, we cannot even **see** the Kingdom of God.

A Wounded Angel Finds Her Way Home

I had spent many years moving in and out of Church. I was filled with feelings of fear, rejection and inadequacy. I was often the victim and object of family controversy and accusations. I was always trying to defend myself and please others. Then one amazing night, a miracle took place in my heart.

At the time, I was struggling in my finances (credit card debt and back taxes), my relationships, especially with my emotions. I was plagued by fear, insecurity, and rejection. I felt so broken and alone, and most of the time I did not feel as if I "belonged" anywhere.

Not knowing which way to turn, I began to attend church with my ex-boyfriend's family in the summer of 1986. His grandmother was especially fond of me and would often pray over me in what I thought then was a strange language. I did not realize that God was gently wooing me to Himself.

One day in church, the pastor told us to go home and read the Book of John. I went home and desperately looked for my mother's Bible. The problem: it was the King James Version and I could not understand it. Then I remembered another book she had that did not look like a Bible at all, but it was – and it was the New Living Translation. Anyway, it was much easier to understand and I began reading it with much enthusiasm.

For several weeks I read the Book of John, until one night in late October I sat up in my bed, with tears streaming down my face, and I said to God, "I believe Jesus is your Son and that He died for me. Please forgive me of all my sins and come into my life." Being alone, I was free to confess out loud all the things for which I wanted forgiveness: an adulterous relationship, drinking, smoking, fornication, and, in general, a life of sin. I do not remember everything I said to Him, but one of the things I remember most about that night is the peace I felt in my heart as I fell asleep. That was November 1, 1986.

I awoke the next morning feeling fully rested, but I felt like I was not finished yet. I had to make an open confession. I did not have a church, so I just chose one. You see, it did not really matter as long I got there and openly confessed my faith in Christ. When the altar call was made, I went up. The following weekend I was baptized as an outward demonstration of my identification with the death, burial, and resurrection of Jesus Christ.

It was a very sober moment for me and I was intensely aware of the decision I had

The Great Commission

made. I belonged to God and His family now and I felt safe for the first time in my life! It would take time to overcome my insecurities and deep feelings of rejection, but already, in my soul, I felt a sigh of relief and a sense of peace that I never knew before. From that day until now, I have never looked back.

The following year, 1987, I moved on to attend a charismatic, inter-denominational church, with a strong teaching ministry. I grew in wisdom, stature, and in favor with God and man for thirteen wonderful years. During my new member studies, I received the Baptism of the Holy Spirit, in February 1988, and went on to serve in ministry in the areas of Worship, Prayer and Christian Education. There I studied and my gifts were developed, I was counseled, I served in full-time ministry on staff for six years, and I met and married my husband.

A couple of years before I got married, I recognized and responded to the call of God on my life to be a Minister of the Gospel of Jesus Christ. Like Jesus, the Holy Spirit led me into the wilderness, and so my preparation began.

It has been twenty-eight years now of walking with and serving the Lord. It has not always been easy; in fact, there have been some really hard times, but I am living proof that God can take a wounded and broken heart and bring healing and restoration for my good and for His glory!

It has been an amazing journey and I am going on to see what the end shall be! I solicit your prayers as I move forward in this new season of end-time purpose.

My name is Angela M. Gracey
and this is my testimony.

Selah

The Great Commission

Prepare the Way

Write out your personal testimony in a format that is easy to pass on to those whom the Lord would lead. Do not make it so short that one cannot fully appreciate your journey, or so long that you lose your point. Use your answers to the three questions below as your outline. Look at some tracts in a Christian bookstore or, perhaps, review the written testimonies of people close to you–your family, friends, or pastors. Be creative in your presentation; most importantly, be honest and sincere in your content.

- *What was your life like before you accepted the Lord as your Savior?*
- *How did you come to receive Jesus as Lord and Savior?*
- *How has your life changed after salvation?*

The Prayer of a Way Maker

"Then He said to His disciples, "The harvest is plentiful but the workers are few. Ask the Lord of the harvest, therefore, to send out workers into His harvest field."
(Matt. 9:37-38)

He told them, "The harvest is plentiful, but the workers are few. Ask the Lord of the harvest, therefore, to send out workers into his harvest field. (Luke 10:2)

Like Jesus, we will emerge from the wilderness of our own season of preparation, anointed and equipped to minister to a lost and dying world. We will have cultivated a lifestyle of worship and prayer. Replenished and restored, we will have received wisdom, instruction, direction that can only come from the inner life of solitude. It is in the secret place of solitude and silence that our message is clarified and perfected.

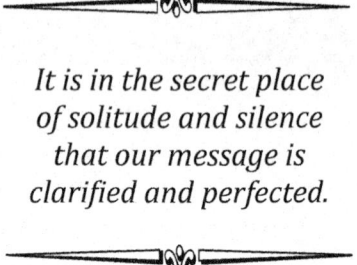

> *It is in the secret place of solitude and silence that our message is clarified and perfected.*

The Secret Life of the Way Maker

Paul says we are to look upon the lost, not with judgment, but with compassion – like Christ (2 Cor. 5:16-17). When it comes to discipleship and developing leaders, compassion and patience are our most valuable tools of ministry. Paul admonishes us that we cannot view the lost only in light of their present condition; we must see them as worthy of salvation through Jesus Christ.

Compassion is the secret ingredient that fuels our message. This transformation takes place in the furnace of solitude and prayer.

There is something about an encounter with Jesus that changes us forever. When we encounter Him – whether at the point of salvation, in healing, or in deliverance – we get a fresh revelation of **who** He is, which changes us for the better.

When God uses us in the ministry of reconciliation, the anointing on our lives invites continuous supernatural experiences: salvations, healings, or deliverances. These experiences, when ordained by the Spirit of God, will always bear fruit in the lives of the touched individuals. *There will be a change in attitude, perspective, vision, and relationship; most importantly, there will be a **change**.*

One important fact: in the lives of new disciples, complete change is not always immediate; they need valuable time to grow and make mistakes. Even in the lives of seasoned disciples, change and growth are vital. As we begin to walk in the newness of life, mistakes are inevitable; however, the frequency of our blunders should decrease as we submit to the guidance of the Holy Spirit.

How do we continue in this new life? In the words of Dr. John C. Maxwell, an internationally recognized author and speaker,

"People do not care how much you know until they know how much you care." Dr. Maxwell is right. Because our fleshly and sinful human nature is inherently selfish, it is difficult for us to readily extend the compassion and patience of Christ without the help of the Holy Spirit – and solitude. The following is an excerpt from a book review that I wrote, highlighting the importance of this aspect of the inner life.

The Role of Solitude and Silence in Ministry

The author begins with a description of the world we live in–a world full of hatred and violence within and outside of our nation. This most excellent work effectively and compellingly seeks to answer some key questions that are foremost in my heart and mind: "What does it mean to be a minister in such a situation? What is required of men and women who want to bring light into the darkness, 'to proclaim good news to the poor ... to proclaim freedom for the prisoners and recovery of sight for the blind, to set the oppressed free, to proclaim the year of the Lord's favor' (Luke 4:18-19)? How can we expect to remain full of creative vitality, of zeal for the Word of God, of desire to serve, and of motivation to inspire our often-numb congregations? Where are we supposed to find nurturing and strength? How can we alleviate our own spiritual hunger and thirst?"

When I pondered these questions, I began to feel overwhelmed

> *Early in my walk, solitude was something I valued highly although I would not have known how to articulate its value or benefits to someone else. I just knew that I needed solitude.*

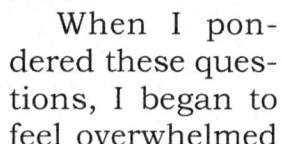

and wondered if I could really be effective for God. I felt my own weakness and sense of inadequacy. My mind took a few steps back in my spiritual journey to see what had kept me on fire for the things of God and when I faltered, what allowed me to get back on track. What I see are times of solitude or isolation – times of little or no activity – spending time alone with God. Early in my walk, solitude was something I valued highly although I would not have known how to articulate its value or benefits to someone else. I just knew that I needed solitude.

In those days, I read a book entitled, **"Hearing God's Voice"** by Henry and Richard Blackaby.[3] I was not able to find it as a reference for this paper, but it was about contemplative prayer and it was one of my most treasured possessions. Although I was a member of a strong teaching and prayer ministry, solitude and contemplation were not taught. We were taught to "speak the Word." So, I was raised to think that unless I was saying something, my prayers were not going anywhere and, of course, if they were not going anywhere, I could not expect an answer.

I continue to welcome those seasons in my life when I have a chance to pull back, reassess, get quiet, read, and pray. As I look back, without those times, I probably would have perished spiritually. The central theme of **"The Way of the Heart – Connecting with God through Prayer, Wisdom and Silence"** by Henri J. M. Nouwen[4] is to call us back to solitude, silence, and prayer as the very lifelines to our spiritual health and effectiveness. I will focus on solitude and silence more, but we will touch on all three.

The author's source of inspiration for us is the *Apophthegmata Patrum: Sayings of the Desert Fathers*. The Desert Fathers lived in the Egyptian desert during the fourth and fifth centuries. Their lives in the desert offer us a unique perspective on ministry life in the twenty-first century. [For example,] Abba Arsenius was encouraged by God to "flee from the world and...be saved." We will discover the "three ways to prevent the world from shaping us into its image and thus three ways to enter life in the spirit."

Solitude

The first thing that strikes me about the lifestyle of the Desert Fathers is that they would withdraw to the desert for a period of twenty years! What a stark contrast to our current society, where we have a problem being quiet for five minutes!

The author uses St. Anthony, the "father of monks," as an example. Again, the thing that makes me want to hang my head is the discipline with which these men lived. Some people are naturally gifted to start something, stick with it, and finish it. Although I have done that too, I usually have to work hard at it. My seasons of solitude were not self-imposed, but rather super-imposed due to unemployment or illness. But the outcomes were still the same. I have found that my experiences were very much the same as St. Anthony's.

As ministers in this compulsive, secular world, the only way we are going to be effective is to cultivate solitude. We need time away. Jesus, during His earthly ministry, always retreated to a mountain or hill for alone time with the Father. According to the text, our very lives depend on it! The blessing of this book is that someone beautifully articulated what takes place in solitude. I would like to share some observations from one of my own experiences.

The Furnace of Transformation

Let me give you context for the season I was in. We had just relocated from [Philadelphia, Pennsylvania to Silver Spring, Maryland]. I had to close my business and start over with no job, no business, and no prospects. I felt an extreme sense of loss and I seemed to be questioning everything I had done. [As the days turned into weeks, I began to seek God. Like St. Anthony, one of the first things that happened was all of my public, personal, and superficial securities

The Prayer of a Way Maker

---

fell off. At first, it was really a relief. I kind of sighed and settled down a little bit. I called it decompression. Then something started to happen on the inside and it did not feel good. Issues that I had been struggling with began to come to the surface and God began to put His supernatural scalpel to the wounds. It was time for me to face the enemy of my soul. Boy, did it hurt]!

There were no friends, no family, no telephone calls, no meetings, no appointments, no workshops or speaking engagements, no training sessions – nothing! It was just me, naked, weak, vulnerable, broken, and humbled before God. When God wants to deal with us, He knows just how to do it. Author, Henri Nouwen says solitude is not necessarily "a private, therapeutic place. Rather, it is the place of conversion, **the place where the old self dies and the new self is born**; the place where the emergence of the new man and the new woman occurs." Solitude is a place of struggle.

Now, according to the Nouwen, it is at this point, that if you and I do not persevere and stay with it, we are going to lose the spiritual benefit. I had no problem hearing God speak. While I did not like what I was hearing, the point is, *I was hearing it*! I humbled myself and submitted to God; meaning, I confessed my sins and repented. As soon as I did that, the enemy fled. He was no longer able to torture me by replaying the

The Way Makers

same old nightmares in my mind and in my dreams.

This brings me to another important observation of "the struggle." Nouwen says "anyone who wants to fight his demons with his own weapons is a fool. Only Christ can overcome the powers of evil. Only in and through Him can we survive the trials of our solitude." This is a direct confirmation of my experience. The Word of God says, "Submit yourselves, then, to God. Resist the devil, and he will flee from you" (James 4:7). As soon as I surrendered to Christ in repentance, the burden and the assault lifted.

My encounter with God led me to repentance, according to His tender mercy and I was restored. Then, something else came up. Ouch! That hurt a lot! More tears, more pain. After weeks of prayer and surrender of my will to His, there was peace.

I want to point out the goal of solitude is not just to confront the assault of the enemy of our soul, but to have a real, bona fide encounter with our Lord Jesus. When we encounter Him, all things are possible. "Thou wilt shew me the path of life: in thy presence is fullness of joy; at thy right hand there are pleasures for evermore" (Psalm 16:11). In His presence we find healing, comfort, encouragement, and strength.

When I emerged from that season of solitude, like St. Anthony, I was healed, restored, and made whole. The key is total surrender

The Prayer of a Way Maker

to God. Like St. Anthony, I emerged with an anointing on my life that I did not even recognize until I accepted a new position at a troubled organization. God used me mightily in that place and opened other doors of opportunity as well. A deep work was wrought in me that solidified my identity in Christ, confirmed my value and worth to God, and brought me to a deeper place of intimacy with Him. The most important thing we can do in this process is to **stay the course**. We will come forth as pure gold.

Silence

While I was reading *"The Way of the Heart: Connecting with God through Prayer, Wisdom, and Silence"* and *"The Supernatural Power of the Transformed Mind"*, by Bill Johnson[5], I was also studying and teaching from a book entitled, *"Hearing God: 30 Different Ways"* by Larry Kreider[6]. One of things we learn quickly in this study is God speaks through His Word in a "still, small voice." The only way to hear the "still, small voice" is to be quiet. Thus, silence plays a major role in hearing the voice of God.

The Incubator of Transformation

I was teaching the lesson on "God Speaks through His Silence," As soon as I turned the page, I gasped because of the agreement in the Spirit! You guessed it: Kreider was speaking the same language! He admonished us that sometimes we do not hear God because we are not paying attention. His silence is actually a signal that He is trying to get our attention. For that we must be quiet. Kreider goes on to say, "*God's silence may occur when He is poised to do His deepest work in our lives.*"[6]

> "God's silence may occur when He is poised to do His deepest work in our lives."[6]

God's silence can remind us of how desperately we need Him. Kreider offers this insight: "*When He is silent and life seems dark, it often motivates us to place our full trust in God. We pay more attention when we are lost in the woods! God may be building our character so we can be more effective in His Kingdom.*"[6] I have said many times, even by way of personal testimony, we hear God in the desert!

The Place of Revelation

Kreider puts it this way: "*God's silence will **reveal** our true attitudes toward God by showing us what is really in our hearts and then giving us the opportunity to fully trust in His power as we persevere.*"[6] The benefits and spiritual blessings come when we hang in there and let patience have its perfect work.

Silence teaches us to depend on God, to wait on and trust Him, and to how prepare for the storms of life. In these last days, we are going to need insulation in our inner lives to be effective [witnesses in an increasingly dark world]. *"...roots grow deep into the earth during times of drought to find water to give the tree a better foundation. Times of God's silence prepare us for future storms."*[6]

Compassionate Ministry

After my season in ["Sanctuary"] I noticed a difference in the way I related to people. Things that once disturbed me greatly no longer affected my disposition. I had acquired a holy boldness – I was not rash or abrasive, but direct and sincere. There was gentleness in the way I responded to all kinds of people and circumstances. The sarcasm was gone. The anger was gone. The need to protect myself (the "me against them" syndrome) disappeared. I noticed a sincere empathy for the plight of those who sought my advice and, finally, my level of influence increased in a way that totally surprised me. All of sudden, it seemed that what I said mattered. When I came out of [the "Sanctuary"] God tested me. But I trusted

Him and emerged victorious through the One who always fights my battles!

I am a more compassionate minister now and that was a major work of transformation and preparation for me, especially as I travel in ministry and minister to the needs of our congregation at the Altar every Sunday! *"Compassion is the fruit of solitude and the foundation of all ministry. The purification and transformation that take place in solitude manifest themselves in compassion."*[4] Nouwen

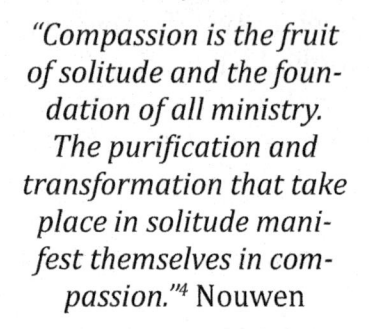

Developing the discipline of setting aside time to commune with God has to be a priority if we are to survive and be effective in these last days. *"Without such a desert we will lose our own soul while preaching the gospel to others. But with such a spiritual abode, we will become increasingly conformed to Him in whose Name we minister."*[3] Nouwen

The Prayer of the Way Maker

Before we move forward, let us pause for a moment, asking the Father to work in us and bring healing – right now. Turn off the TV, radio, phone, computer, and any other distractions. Find a quiet place to pray. Then, turn your heart to the Father and pray with me:

Heavenly Father, I thank You for the gift of eternal life through Your Son, Jesus Christ. I thank You that I am Your workmanship, created in Christ Jesus to fulfill the calling that you have placed on my life. Thank You for the gift of Your Holy Spirit, who is my teacher, leading and guiding me into all truth, while equipping me to do the work of the ministry. Just like the Nation of Israel, Your will is that I be emotionally and spiritually healthy as well as whole before I step into all that You have for me.

So Father, who art in Heaven, hallowed be Your Name, Your Kingdom come, Your will be done, on earth, in my life, as it is in Heaven. Give me this day my daily bread– Your divine provision, protection, and divine health; all that I need to fulfill the plans and purposes for my life; all that I need to meet the demands of the day–and forgive me of my trespasses as I forgive those who have trespassed against me. It is my desire to walk humbly before You and to do good. Search me, O God; try me and know my anxious thoughts and see if there be any wicked way in me and lead in the way everlasting. Then I will confess my sins–every word, thought, and deed that is not pleasing to You. It is against You and You alone that I have sinned and done that which is evil in Your sight. Create in me a clean heart, and renew a right spirit within me. Cast me not away from Your presence; please do not take Your spirit from me; restore to me the joy of my salvation, so I may worship You.

Thank You, Father, that You do not deal with me according to my sins, nor reward me according to my iniquities. You are merciful and gracious, slow to anger, and plenteous in mercy. Because I have confessed my sins, You are faithful and just to forgive me and to cleanse me of all unrighteousness.

Lead me not into temptation, but with every temptation, make a way of escape as You have promised, and deliver me from the evil one–the enemy of my soul. I walk after the spirit and not after the flesh. I take every thought captive and bring it under obedience to Jesus Christ. I have the mind of Christ.

Father, thank You that You lead and guide me into all truth by Your Spirit, and You satisfy my mouth with good things! You restore my soul. I walk in divine health, physically, emotionally, and spiritually. Your Word renews my mind; by Your stripes, I am healed!

The Prayer of a Way Maker

Though I walk through the valley of the shadow of death, I will fear no evil. I boldly walk by faith and on purpose to fulfill my end-time assignment. I am a Way Maker, called to prepare the Way for Your return. I know that You are with me wherever I go, and nothing can separate me from Your love. I am an Ambassador for Christ and I declare that I can do all things through Christ who strengthens me; it is You who equipped and approved me.

Thank you for working in me both to will and to do Your good pleasure. I know that Your plans for me are good, so I look forward to the future without fear. I bless You, Lord, with all my soul and I bless Your Holy Name, with all that is within me. Amen, Amen, and Amen!

The Commissioning of a Way Maker

(A Prophetic Word from the Lord)

"Beloved,

I have summoned you **by name** (Isa. 43:1).

As the Father sent Me, **I am sending you** (John 20:21).

You did not choose me, but I **chose you and appointed you**... (John 15:16).

But you...my servant...whom I have chosen, you descendants of Abraham my friend, (Isa. 41:8).

I took you from the ends of the earth; from its farthest corners I called you. I said, **'You are my servant'**; **I have chosen you and have not rejected you** (Isa. 41:9).

So **do not fear**, for I am with you; do not be dismayed, for I am your God. **I will strengthen you and help you**; I will uphold you with my righteous right hand (Isa. 41:10).

All who rage against you will surely be ashamed and disgraced; those who oppose you will be as nothing and perish (Isa. 41:11).

Though you search for your enemies, you will not find them. Those who wage war against you will be as **nothing at all** (Isa. 41:12).

For I am the LORD, your God, who **takes hold of your right hand** and says to you, '**Do not fear; I will help you**' (Isa. 41:13).

'Do not be afraid, O worm Jacob, O little Israel, for **I myself will help you**,' declares the LORD, **your Redeemer**, the Holy One of Israel (Isa. 41:14).

'...Therefore **go** and **make disciples of all nations**, baptizing them in the name of the Father and of the Son and of the Holy Spirit, and teaching them to obey everything I have commanded you. And surely **I am with you always**, to the very end of the age' (Matt. 28:19-20).

Amen, Amen, and Amen."

Selah

PART TWO

PREPARING THE WAY OF THE LORD: IN THE HOUSE OF THE LORD

"Now when the queen of Sheba heard of the fame of Solomon concerning the name of the LORD, she came to test him with hard questions. She came to Jerusalem with a very great retinue, with camels that bore spices, very much gold, and precious stones; and when she came to Solomon, she spoke with him about all that was in her heart. So Solomon answered all her questions; there was nothing so difficult for the king that he could not explain it to her. And when the queen of Sheba had seen all the wisdom of Solomon, the house that he had built, the food on his table, the seating of his servants, the service of his waiters and their apparel, his cupbearers, and his entryway by which he went up to the house of the LORD, there was no more spirit in her. Then she said to the king: "It was a true report which I

heard in my own land about your words and your wisdom. However I did not believe the words until I came and saw with my own eyes; and indeed the half was not told me. Your wisdom and prosperity exceed the fame of which I heard. Happy are your men and happy are these your servants, who stand continually before you and hear your wisdom! Blessed be the L<small>ORD</small> *your God, who delighted in you, setting you on the throne of Israel! Because the* L<small>ORD</small> *has loved Israel forever, therefore He made you king, to do justice and righteousness." Then she gave the king one hundred and twenty talents of gold, spices in great quantity, and precious stones. There never again came such abundance of spices as the queen of Sheba gave to King Solomon."* (1 Kings 10:1-10)

INTRODUCTION

In this part of our discussion, I want to share a testimony that became the catalyst for birthing a new dimension of the vision God has given me: **Developing leaders to prepare the way of the Lord in the House of God.** Our main text reveals the anointing and prosperity that comes to the House of God that is set in order. It is the principle on which this section of the book rests.

But first, I want to make a distinction in terms: spiritually speaking, we are all God's "house"; meaning, God, by His Spirit, makes His home in us. We are the Body of Christ. That was the first part of the book. However, in this part of our talk, when I speak of "house", I am referring to the place of your ministry, non-profit organization or business establishment. I'm referring to the physical place where you operate and carry out the work of business and the work of the ministry.

As Way Makers – **Ambassadors of Christ** – preparing **the way** of the Lord, we have been commissioned to not only preach the Gospel, but to "make disciples". (Matt. 28:18) To do that, we need to provide and maintain a stable environment for the end-time harvest of souls. Jesus said in His priestly prayer (John 17) that all that the Father gave Him are His and not one of them is lost (*paraphrased*). As His Ambassadors, we must make the same declaration that none of those whom the Father gives us are lost. We cannot lose them because we failed to provide a safe, nurturing environment for them to grow and serve.

Thom Rainer and Chuck Lawless conducted a Healthy Church Survey[7] in which 160 questions were asked to assess the condition of the Church in the 6 key purposes of the Church (worship, evangelism, discipleship, ministry, prayer and fellowship). They reported on the most common responses to areas of weakness. I find this one to be most insightful:

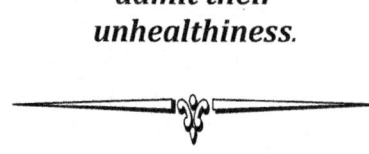

> *Many churches admit their unhealthiness.*

Many churches admit their unhealthiness. By far, churches that complete our survey perceive themselves as

Introduction

"marginally unhealthy" or "unhealthy." To be fair, these churches contact us because they have already recognized their need for help (which, many other needy churches do not recognize), but our process is easier because of their own admission.[7]

My passion for them runs deeper than a mere acknowledgement of my responsibility as a Minister of the Gospel. There is an apostolic call on my life to institute His system of order into the government of the Church and the affairs of man. It took me a long time to recognize and acknowledge that God has used me throughout my life to set things in order. In every organization, I started in a position where there was no system or structure. I could see what wasn't working, and was able to discern and facilitate change, often in the midst of strong opposition.

In the next few chapters I will address these issues and expose the absolute necessity and responsibility we have to provide a safe place. Scripture says what we have learned, the same commit to faithful men (and women). That is what I will attempt to do here. I want to make it clear that I do not consider myself to have attained perfection (although "perfection" is not what is required), nor do I esteem myself higher than anyone else. But, I am accountable;

The Way Makers

when I know better, I have to do better. He who knows to do right and doesn't do it, is in sin! (James 4:17) Woe to the person who falls prey to a leader who does not hold himself accountable to anyone!

Woe to the person who falls prey to a leader who does not hold himself accountable to anyone!

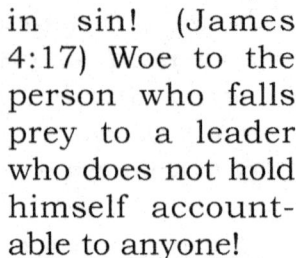

I certainly don't have all the answers; but might I suggest that we take the offensive. If, as Way Makers, we cultivate a healthy fear of the Lord and take heed to what the Spirit of the Lord is saying, we would walk very circumspectly, as wise, and implement Godly order and healthy leadership authority. If those who are trying to live half way right are on shaky ground, how much more those who ignore God's warning? (Heb. 12:25 *paraphrased*)

Some valuable lessons came out of this experience: speaking truth to power, biblical boundaries, exercising your God-given authority, the changing of the guard, the corruption of selfish ambition, protecting the anointing on your life and ministry, and the absolute necessity for structure and order in every organization, but especially in the House of God. I believe they will edify, strengthen and prepare you as you develop into the Way Maker you are called to be.

The Changing of the Guard

The next day John was there again with two of his disciples. When he saw Jesus passing by, he said, "Look, the Lamb of God!" When the two disciples heard him say this, they followed Jesus. Turning around, Jesus saw them following and asked, "What do you want?" They said, "Rabbi" (which means "Teacher"), "where are you staying?" "Come," he replied, "and you will see." So they went and saw where he was staying, and they spent that day with him. It was about four in the afternoon. Andrew, Simon Peter's brother, was one of the two who heard what John had said and who had followed Jesus. The first thing Andrew did was to find his brother Simon and tell him, "We have found the Messiah" (that is, the Christ). And he brought him to Jesus. John 1:35-42

The Changing of the Guard

God is repositioning for the culmination of all things. Before the end comes, the Gospel must be preached to everyone. He is positioning His Ambassadors: Way Makers called to prepare the way of the Lord, to fulfill their ultimate assignment on earth. Kingdom purposes dictate where we are placed; not our qualifications, skills, talents, experience or expertise. Our position has nothing to do with our education or financial resources, but it is determined by our willingness to be obedient and to complete the assignment. The kingdoms of this world are about to become the Kingdom of our God. Way Makers will be strategically placed in positions of government, education, finance, medicine, law and business. Many of us will come out of obscurity and take our God-ordained places – center stage of God's end-time plan! As indicated in our chapter text, many will no longer follow man, but rather follow Jesus and become "fishers of men"!

We are God's House; those who lead in His house (meaning, The Body of Christ), have to be healthy emotionally and spiritually, and perhaps most importantly, possess a healthy fear of the Lord, in order to be prepared to receive and nurture the end-time harvest. There is so much more at stake when we consider the decisions we make and the motives behind them. Those who submit to the work of the Holy Spirit in their lives and are prepared will be raised up; those who are not will be moved out. God is repositioning; if you hold on too tight, destruction will come upon your ministry and there will be no provision. Saul is another example of one being so consumed with jealousy and rage, and being determined to hold on to his throne as King at all costs, that it ultimately led to his death **and** the death of his son, Jonathan.

Stepping Out on Faith

In the past, emerging leaders, especially ministers and pastors, were often mentored and trained by a current or former leader. The mentor relationship often included a combination of practical, spiritual and educational experiences. However, prior to that phase of the relationship, those leaders waited for their gifts to be recognized in the

Church. This may be done in different ways, depending on the Church, but often it was through public declaration of gifting or office, the "laying on of hands", anointing and prayer. That's great, and well within spiritual and Church protocol.

However, greed, pride, insecurity and selfish ambition often prevent many leaders from recognizing and developing potential leaders. We all must go through the season of preparation and testing between the call and the manifestation; however, the fulfillment of the promise is directly related to how well we respect spiritual authority, submit to the process, and respond in obedience.

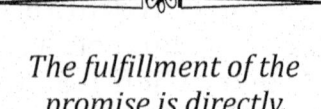

> *The fulfillment of the promise is directly related to how well we respect spiritual authority, submit to the process, and respond in obedience.*

More often than not, this is where we get stuck. We are waiting on recognition and approval for those in spiritual authority over us. We wait on opportunities to serve in our place of worship. When those opportunities don't materialize or are cut off, we become discouraged and attempt to take matters into our own hands. God is saying resist the temptation. Your time will come. There will be a "changing of the guard".

I want to encourage you today not to give up. Submit to the preparation process. Humble yourself before God and He will exalt you in due season. God knows; He will lead you in the way you should go. As long as the earth remains, there will be seed time and harvest. You have seed in the ground. You will reap what you've sown if you faint not. Due season always comes!

The vision is yet for an appointed time. Any time is good for the ungodly; but for Way Makers there is *"an appointed time"* to act. In this hour, it is critical that we have "ears to hear" what God is saying. Just prior to manifestation is the *season of waiting*–waiting for instructions. (Isa. 40:31) It's often the season when God heals the wounds of preparation. He establishes, restores and strengthens us for our next assignment. In the fullness of time, the inner work is complete and it is time to step out. When God says "move", you move!

The Assignment against Your Assignment–Spiritual Warfare

When God promotes us to the next level, it requires us to begin to move into a higher degree of spiritual discernment. Spiritual warfare is often so strong that success will not feel like success at all. We will often feel like we are suffering one set back after another. That's because the opposition is greater. Take heart; in this life there will be persecution. Jesus said, "I have overcome the world." Greater is He that's in you, than he that is in the world!

"A great door and effectual is open unto me and there are many adversaries." (1 Cor. 16:9)

Have you ever prayed and declared the Word of God over your life and circumstances, only to have things go from bad to worse? Did you step out in faith in obedience to God, only to encounter one obstacle after another? Have you ever encountered opposition so strong that you begin to wonder if you ever heard God at all? I have. I have experienced all of these and the conflicting emotions and inner turmoil that often comes with these questions. But I've discovered one thing: the problem isn't that I did something wrong or that I didn't have faith; I did. The problem was my *perspective*. How did I see and process the opposition I was experiencing? And more importantly, how would I respond? God has answered my prayer, and I'd like to share the revelation with you.

Sometimes chaos and difficult circumstances are evidence of our faith being mixed with the Word of God we received. You see, it's not our lack of faith. Quite the contrary; we really do believe God! It's

because of our faith that spiritual warfare ensues. So often, the challenge for us is to determine if we believe God enough to provoke us to act on what we believe–no matter how crazy and desperate things look.

A great door and effectual is open to us, but there are many adversaries. We think those adversaries look like us: flesh and blood; but that is how we are deceived by the enemy of our souls. The facts may say one thing, but the "truth" is our adversaries manifest in the form of:

Distractions	False Accusation	Anxiety
Criticism	Illness	Busyness
Workplace Conflict	Financial Crisis	Intimidation
Discouragement	Fear	Temptation to Quit

In the passage, it is clear that we are not left to our own defenses. God has given us the weapons of our warfare, and they are mighty through God to destroy every stronghold and bring the enemy to his wicked knees! The thing to remember is that in this battle, we can never let our guard down–not in this day and time. The older I get, the more I realize that being "out of uniform" can be most costly to my God-given assignment.

I've learned that I need to appropriate the whole Armor of God every day in order to walk in victory.

The Weapons of Our Warfare

So I returned to the disciplines of the faith with a renewed passion to seek His face: spending time praying in the Spirit and reading the Word of God; serving Him and His people with my spiritual gifts, giving, and most importantly, spending time in worship and solitude–cultivating His Presence. I began to feed my faith on every occasion; keeping my relationships clear of division/strife or unforgiveness; and living a holy life–seeking first His kingdom and His righteousness.

The scripture says to put on the "full" Armor of God–not just part of it. We have to be fully dressed so that the enemy cannot take advantage of us. That is the key to victory. The attack is certain to come if we dare to **"believe God" and then "act" on what we believe**. In "acting" on what I believe, I've came to realize that it involved risk. I had to trust God for the variables that I couldn't see or control. It was uncomfortable for me to make some of the decisions I had to make. Standing for righteousness meant I had to take a stand without regard for my personal circumstances, and I intended to do just that. May God get all of the Glory!

When the inner turmoil stops, the peace of God is made manifest. Then you will know what to do.

Beloved, you can't stop or prevent spiritual warfare. It comes with the territory; but, you can take the offensive by being prepared for the attack. Don't let the enemy steal your time, talent and resources! If you've gotten off track, ask God for wisdom and refocus. Dare to trust Him no matter what it looks like. He will restore and redirect your path (Prov. 3:5-6). Submit to God; the devil must flee.

When the inner turmoil stops, the peace of God is made manifest. Then you will know what to do.

The Attraction of Distractions

Distraction is a subtle, yet deadly tool of the enemy because it steals your time. Time once it is lost, cannot be recovered. It is the most valuable commodity of life. God can redeem time by restoring what was lost, but He doesn't reverse time. As much as I might like to, I'll never be 40 again!

When God begins to move you into a new season, an act of war ensues between the "good" thing and the "God" thing. There will be others pulling on your time, talent and resources. It's so subtle. It will be disguised as "collaboration". You will find yourself working on a project that appears to be mutually beneficial; but before you know it, you have spent valuable time and resources that could have – and should have – been spent on the vision God gave "you"! I speak from experience. At the end, I found that the results were nowhere near what I expected or desired. Stay focused! Learn to say "no, thank you." You are on assignment!

Whatever you do, **DON'T GIVE UP!** He will fulfill His purpose for your life! Show up dressed for battle every day and having done all–**STAND!**

A Way Maker in Your Household

*"A deacon must be the husband of but one wife and **must manage his children and his household well. Those who have served well gain an excellent standing and great assurance in their faith in Christ Jesus**. Although I hope to come to you soon, I am writing you these instructions so that, if I am delayed, **you will know how people ought to conduct themselves in God's household, which is the church of the living God**, the pillar and foundation of the truth."* (1Timothy 3:12-15–bold text for emphasis only)

A WAY MAKER IN YOUR HOUSEHOLD

In First Timothy, Paul gives a description of the characteristics of leaders in the Church. Way Makers prepare the way of the Lord first, in their own households. When we give Jesus Lordship over our lifestyle and family relationships, we are then in position to duplicate that lifestyle in the Church, as Paul instructs in the chapter text. Let's look at this more closely.

Managing Your Household

First, I want to bring to your attention to the very first part of verse 12 (bold text for emphasis only): a qualified leader is one who knows how to "***manage*** his ***children and his household*** well." To be skilled in bringing order and structure to God's house, one must be able to govern one's own home. That means there should be a demonstration of the power and presence of Jesus Christ in our homes.

Now, I'm not just referring to how we "keep house" necessarily, but that is certainly important; but a more excellent way might be revealed in whether or not we have Godly priorities. Are husbands loving and cherishing their wives as Christ loved the Church? Are wives honoring, respecting and submissive to their husbands? Are we raising our children in the fear and admonition of the Lord? Do we honor God with the first fruits of our increase? In other words, is Jesus Christ Lord of your home? If the answer is yes, then the manifestation of that will be seen in your conduct, your relationships with each other, and the physical appearance of your home.

Paul says if you've mastered home management – if you have established "order" in your home, then you are now qualified to bring order to God's house.

Excellent Standing and Assurance of Faith

Second, I want to point out the benefits that one derives from establishing order in one's life and household: "***excellent standing*** and great ***assurance of faith*** in Christ Jesus." When we honor God and put Him first, He is most pleased. Obedience pleases God, and when we are obedient, we have assurance of faith, that God will honor His Word and His promises to us. He said, "No good thing would He withhold from those who walk uprightly before Him." In other words, when establishing Godly priorities and order in our lives, we gain God's favor and blessing.

Our light shines when we have order and the anointing on our lives and ministry flows unhindered.

Our light shines when we have order and the anointing on our lives and ministry flows unhindered. It is a witness and testimony to the world, and therein is the Father glorified!

Proper Conduct in God's House

And finally, Paul says *"you will know how people ought to conduct themselves in God's household".* The implication here is that managing our homes well, not only prepares us, but *qualifies* us to conduct ourselves properly in God's house. There is a right and a wrong way to conduct ourselves in God's household. There is a criterion for selecting leaders and if we do it correctly, we will execute the duties of our position or office with care, diligence and obedience to God. Those who serve well gain an excellent standing and assurance of faith, the Church is managed by capable leadership, and God is glorified. These words were written for your instruction.

Way Makers in the House of God

"Here is a trustworthy saying: Whoever aspires to be an overseer desires a noble task. Now the overseer is to be above reproach, faithful to his wife, temperate, self-controlled, respectable, hospitable, able to teach, not given to drunkenness, not violent but gentle, not quarrelsome, not a lover of money. He must manage his own family well and see that his children obey him, and he must do so in a manner worthy of full respect. (If anyone does not know how to manage his own family, how can he take care of God's church?) He must not be a recent convert, or he may become conceited and fall under the same judgment as the devil. He must also have a good reputation with outsiders, so that he will not fall into disgrace and into the devil's trap. In

the same way, deacons are to be worthy of respect, sincere, not indulging in much wine, and not pursuing dishonest gain. They must keep hold of the deep truths of the faith with a clear conscience. They must first be tested; and then if there is nothing against them, let them serve as deacons. In the same way, the women are to be worthy of respect, not malicious talkers but temperate and trustworthy in everything."
(1Timothy 3:1-11)

WAY MAKERS IN THE HOUSE OF GOD

So many leaders are being exposed in moral failure after moral failure: from pedophilia, adultery, fornication to homosexuality. No surprise there. God said judgment is coming first, to the household of faith. In all of its forms, it has taken a devastating toll on the Body of Christ. People's lives have been destroyed and many have pulled away from or have left the Church altogether. I've witnessed this myself – up close and personal and the fallout has birthed a passion in me to reach those who have left the faith. I do love God's people and I believe as an Ambassador of Christ, it is my duty to call them back to the fold.

Let me pause for a moment to say that I have served under some amazing leaders. Each of the Pastors I've served under as a leader, has made a significant deposit in my life as a Christian and as a leader. Now of course they are not perfect, but then perfection was not what I expected. Despite their flaws, I am the minister I am today because of their leadership and service; not to mention, the many lives that were claimed for the Kingdom of God. My growth and development yielded some very valuable lessons, and my intention is to give you the benefit of my lessons learned, because at some point in your growth and development as a leader, you will need them. Allow me to share a brief testimony:

I served as a Human Resources professional in full-time ministry for a little more than 15 years, and as a manager in the non-profit sector for almost 5 years. During that time, twice, I experienced the fallout of moral failure on the part of senior leadership. The effects were devastating for many, including my husband and me. As a Human Resources professional, I was directly affected by moral misconduct, when one employee accused a senior leader of inappropriate touching, and another employee accused the same leader of inappropriately touching her son! This called for a professional response, and as a Minister of the Gospel, there was also a demand for a spiritual response.

As the only in-house authority on personnel matters and employee relations, my position was seriously compromised. I had an obligation to be supportive and an advocate for the injured party (and rightfully so); however, doing so appeared to be disloyal to management (Pastoral leadership) to whom I was also accountable and functioned as a supportive partner. Conversely, I certainly couldn't support or uphold moral misconduct – as an employee, a leader or as a Minister of the Gospel! Notwithstanding, there was the possibility of more severe consequences, should legal action ensued. That action and the timing of that action suddenly made things very, very clear and I knew exactly what I had to do.

My husband and I continued to worship God and serve Him and His people, but our service to God was marred by those experiences and they became the catalyst for this area of my ministry.

They painfully reveal what can happen when our leaders are not healed in certain areas, and the consequences of not having the proper structure in place to guide leadership/ management responses and decisions. If you are in a major leadership role, my goal here is to share some principles and observations with you that will help you to make wise decisions and take a stand for righteousness.

When there has been a breach in Godly conduct on the part of leadership, it is important to first remember that you are not judge and jury. We are all vulnerable to sin. The Bible says, "If any man thinks he stands firm, let him be careful not to fall." (1 Cor. 10:12 paraphrased) However, just because we have all sinned and fallen short of the glory of God, does not mean that we are not to biblically confront sin, especially among leadership. There are souls hanging in the balance! It is important that we take orderly, but immediate action. Gather the facts: as much information as possible before making any kind of decision. Once you have as clear an understanding as possible of what happened, the next step is to take it to God in prayer and seek biblical and Godly counsel. Finally, respond within your realm of Godly authority, and within biblical and spiritual boundaries.

How we respond is more important than the infraction itself. The bible says we are to confront one overtaken in a fall and "restore them gently." The goal is restoration and redemption. We are to go to them in humility – not with a haughty spirit. When it comes to leadership, the Bible gives specific direction as in 1Timothy 5:19-21:

> *"Do not entertain an accusation against an elder unless it is brought by two or three witnesses. But those elders who are sinning you are to reprove before everyone, so that the others may take warning. I charge you, in the sight of God and Christ Jesus and the elect angels, to keep these instructions without partiality, and to do nothing out of favoritism."*

As I said, make sure the accusation has solid footing before you confront, and when you do, go in the spirit of humility, with the goal of repentance and restoration. God sent Ezekiel to confront the nation of Israel about their sin. It was a very difficult assignment, but God told him that they were rebellious and stubborn, but he was not to be afraid of them or their words. God told him to confront Israel – "You shall speak My words to them," whether they listen or not. (Ez. 2:1-8). Such were the words God gave me to speak; and I responded in obedience. If you are in a position of leadership, God will also require you to do the same at some point.

My experience raises some very important questions in light of our Kingdom calling as Way Makers:

- How are we going to nurture and care for those coming into The Kingdom?
- Can we provide a safe place for nurture, edification and growth?
- What do you do when those in authority are weak and compromised by their own selfish ambition?
- How do you protect the newborn in Christ or the spiritually fragile and admonish those in authority at the same time?

I've discovered there are some powerful truths and valuable principles from which we can glean, having walked through this experience. I believe there are some essential character traits that God is looking for in those who are called to *prepare the way of the Lord*. Not only should we submit to God's training in this area, but we should also instill and teach the same to faithful men and women of God.

Way Makers in the household of faith are called to:

- **Speak Truth to Power**. I knew I had a responsibility to speak truth to the situation and the offending party; I was well within my sphere of authority as the Human Resources Officer. Despite manipulative efforts, I was determined to respond according to God's leading

– not that of others, and not my own. God said to speak the truth with gentleness, firmness and respect. This was one time I chose not to react, but to carefully examine my own thoughts and feelings and then take responsible action. As one who struggles with co-dependent behavior, this was extremely important for me. So I sought the Lord.

As I struggled with how to hear God for what He wanted me to do in that situation, He led me to a scripture in Ezekiel 2:5-8 (NIV):

> *"As for them, whether they hear or whether they refuse – for they are a rebellious house – yet they will know that a prophet has been among them. And you, son of man, do not be afraid of them nor be afraid of their words, though briers and thorns are with you and you dwell among scorpions; do not be afraid of their words or dismayed by their looks, though they are a rebellious house. You shall speak My words to them, whether they hear or whether they refuse, for they are rebellious. But you, son of man, hear what I say to you. Do not be rebellious like that rebellious house; open your mouth and eat what I give you."*

In the scripture notes I was admonished to speak gently and respectfully, but to speak nonetheless. That is exactly what I did. I believe I was led of the Lord because the scriptures direct us when we have a conflict with our brother, to go to him directly and bring it to his attention, and if he receives it, you have won your brother. I did receive a response – a phone call – in which the leader seemed very receptive; he said he appreciated my letter and thanked me. I had won my brother.

According to God's instructions to Ezekiel, I am not responsible for what he does with it. My only responsibility was to speak the truth in love. I most certainly forgave him and hold nothing against him; however, forgiveness is not all that is required. We must respond and take a stand for righteousness. It will be a testimony – an example of the believer–for those in the Body of Christ. **We may not be welcomed or accepted, but we will be respected.** Others may compromise to further their own agenda, but Way Makers are to take a stand and address these actions directly and without compromise.

- **Spiritual Boundaries** (Matt. 13:24-30)

Just because we find ourselves in a difficult situation or environment, does not mean

The Way Makers

we are out of the will of God. It is God alone who sets the time for when your assignment begins and when it ends. Our job is to be faithful and steadfast until we are released. Just because there is conflict doesn't mean you are in the wrong place. God will give you grace and the oil of joy to endure and make it through, and a garment of praise for the spirit of heaviness. (Is. 61:1-3) He is working in you **and** in the situation. Iron sharpens iron. God will cause you to triumph if you are not weary in well doing.

Here is what I know: The wheat must grow with the tares. When we are on assignment, it is important to have the "big picture" in mind. It's about the "Body of Christ" and Kingdom purposes. We must walk circumspectly as wise, redeeming the time, and making the most of every opportunity to display Christ. Our responses and actions will affect the Body of Christ. If we make hasty decisions or rash judgments out of emotion, or try to execute justice in our own strength, we run the risk of hurting and bringing spiritual harm to the Body of Christ. In most instances, the Body suffers the most – losing more wheat than tares.

One of the most profound lessons I learned (and you will too) is how to co-exist, cooperate and co-labor in a less than ideal environment. Part of the preparation process will require us to work and serve with people that we don't like and who may not like us. Nonetheless, we have to learn how to get along with each other, respect each other and serve God's people in our area of gifting. My principle mindset was that I was placed there by God on assignment, my gifts had made room for me, and when it was time for my release, my promotion would come from God. I got to know God as my advocate and my defense. No weapon formed against me prospered. God is no respecter of persons. He will do the same for you. Trust Him. Learn your lessons well. He will bring you through. You will not hear His voice during the test; the teacher is always silent during the test; however, when it's over, you will hear His voice. In the fullness of time, He will deliver you.

- ***Recognize That "You" Always Have A Choice*** (Eph. 6:1-10)

One of the key concepts to recognize here is that you cannot change anyone, nor are you responsible for anyone's behavior but your own. If we find ourselves under the authority of those who do not respond in accordance with the scriptures on matters of significance, we **can** do something other than turn a "blind eye". We can report to appropriate authorities, speak truth to power, and having done all, take our stand for God. Actions speak louder than words. I chose to tender my resignation in declaration of the fact that I would not continue to support ungodly behavior on the part of leadership. You may find yourself facing such circumstances in an organization or ministry. How will you respond? I can tell you, if you do not take a stand for Christ, the implications and the consequences can be quite serious in light of your witness and your ability to prepare the way for others to come into the Kingdom.

- ***Exercise Your Authority in the Body of Christ.*** (1 Timothy 5:20-21)

I believe that part of my apostolic calling is to declare the Word of God to those in leadership: to edify, admonish, encourage and warn them. In the situation I described earlier, God gave me a word to speak to those in leadership, and I have to admit, I was afraid. I was only partially obedient. I delivered a respectful, yet firm admonishment and warning to the offending party, but that was not the end of the assignment. I was also to declare a warning to those in supporting leadership roles who neglected their responsibility. I had no peace in my spirit. I felt I had left something undone. There was unfinished business. I returned to my journal and read the scripture that

God directed me to declare. That's when I saw it. It was clear that I was in trouble with God if I did not complete the assignment; so I did – without hesitation. The following is my obedient response:

The scriptures speak clearly as to the consequences for leaders who do not exercise their God-given authority, close their eyes to sin for selfish ambition, and who not only choose to keep silent, but do nothing to enforce boundaries and accountability:

1 Samuel 3:11-18 *(NIV)*

*[11] And the L*ORD *said to Samuel: "See, I am about to do something in Israel that will make the ears of everyone who hears about it tingle. [12] At that time I will carry out against Eli everything I spoke against his family—from beginning to end. [13] For I told him that I would judge his family forever because of the sin he knew about; his sons blasphemed God,[a] and he failed to restrain them. [14] Therefore I swore to the house of Eli, 'The guilt of Eli's house will never be atoned for by sacrifice or offering.'"*

*[15] Samuel lay down until morning and then opened the doors of the house of the L*ORD*. He was afraid to tell Eli the vision, [16] but Eli called him and said, "Samuel, my son."*

Samuel answered, "Here I am."

17 *"What was it he said to you?" Eli asked. "Do not hide it from me. May God deal with you, be it ever so severely, if you hide from me anything he told you." 18 So Samuel told him everything, hiding nothing from him. Then Eli said, "He is the* Lord*; let him do what is good in his eyes."*

Every member, volunteer and employee has a reasonable expectation to be able to bring their family to Church and to serve and worship in a "safe place." When we fail to meet this expectation, we have failed miserably, and God is deeply grieved. Judgment starts with the Household of God. If the governing body of a Church, a school or an organization looks the other way and does not take a biblical stand for righteousness, destruction will come upon that house. Be not deceived; God is not mocked.

So often I hear people – even Christians– express the fact that they feel they have no right to speak to or hold accountable the actions of those in leadership, with this statement as justification: "Let he who is without sin cast the first stone." I find this very disturbing. Just because we have all sinned and fallen short of the glory of God, does not mean that there is to be no standard of accountability! I believe we take the coward's way out when we use that as an excuse. God is holding us accountable just as He did Eli.

The Body of Christ has become so complacent and lukewarm that we lack the moral and spiritual inner fortitude to hold our leaders accountable for their actions – especially ones that are particularly heinous – like child molestation and statutory rape, etc. I might add these are especially despicable to me because these "crimes" involve young, defenseless, vulnerable children and teenagers. It is abhorrent and an abomination in the sight of God!

As I said earlier, this has become pervasive throughout the Church at large and has brought reproach upon the cause of the Kingdom. Our leaders need help, healing and hope. However, when their issues begin to negatively impact the Body of Christ, it is the responsibility of leadership to deal immediately, firmly, in a way that is redemptive, but without compromise. There is just too much at stake.

- ***Making Life Changes***

What I have come to understand about movement in the Kingdom, as it relates to our work – whether in full-time ministry or secular vocation – is that if you are a Christian, taking a promotion or lateral move, tendering a resignation or applying for a new job has far less to do with career

The Way Makers

advancement and salary increases. It has everything to do with God's purposes and our Kingdom assignment, and our obedience and commitment to that assignment. Most importantly, it is discerning the "Kairos" timing of God–**defined as**: a time when conditions are right for the accomplishment of a crucial action; the opportune and decisive moment. Discerning God's timing empowers us to know when the assignment is complete and it's time to move on. More often than not, we often make these decisions without any thought to Kingdom implications.

Sometimes knowing or discerning when to move is the mark of maturity and intimacy in our walk with God. This so important because God is sending the next person to fulfill their assignment. It has nothing to do with whether you were fired or laid off or downsized. No matter how it happens, it is critical that we are able to see the hand of God in the situation so that we can cooperate with His agenda and move with the Spirit. Failing to do so has major implications in the Kingdom and fulfilling our destiny.

There is always a "changing of the guard". Nothing stays the same forever. Like Phillip, who witnessed to the Ethiopian eunuch, God may abruptly move you from one position to another to accomplish an assignment, and when it's done, He will bring that assignment to an immediate close and send you somewhere else! We can accept it when we read it in scripture, but we are challenged with this in our personal lives. We must learn to "end well."

- **_Necessary Endings_**

In life and in ministry, it is important to recognize and be able to handle change. Flexibility and adaptability are essential characteristics of effective Way Makers.

A vital hallmark of a Way Maker is the ability to operate in the realm of reality. It is a sign of maturity. John the Baptist declared, "He must increase and I must decrease." I'm sure he didn't think it would mean his beheading! While he was incarcerated, he began to question whether Jesus was the Messiah or not. Jesus sent word to encourage John not to be offended because of His lack of response to his situation. We aren't told in scripture whether or not John made peace with the reality of his dilemma. I believe he did. I believe one word from Jesus enabled him to endure the situation. Jesus Himself said, "There is none greater than John the Baptist!" (Matt. 11:11 paraphrased) John the Baptist ended well!

To discern when to end something requires that we face the reality of the situation in order to arrive at the "pruning" moment (the moment at which you realize what is no longer working or fruitful in your life, and you are ready to end one thing and start another). Like seasons, when one ends, it signals the start of another. Way Makers recognize endings as a natural part of life. In John 15, Jesus says this is a necessary part of our spiritual life if we are to bear much fruit in the Kingdom of God.

To learn this most valuable lesson and get an understanding to apply it to my life, I read an excellent book entitled **"Necessary Endings"** by Dr. Henry Cloud[8]. I love his work; it has helped me in many ways to improve my spiritual and emotional health. I highly recommend it! According to Dr. Cloud, there are all sorts of mind and behavior patterns that can prevent us from recognizing a "pruning" moment; however, once we get there and we are ready to make a change, Dr. Cloud offers guidelines to follow that will help us to "end well." From his work, I'd like to share nine ways to determine whether there is hope to remain or whether change is indeed necessary. I used these same guidelines when I reached the pruning moment in my life (paraphrased for quick summary):

1. "There should be verifiable involvement in a proven change process; e.g., rehab, counseling, or training.
2. Additional structure implemented; e.g., set-in-stone times and activities

that are not dependent upon the person's whims, schedule or preferences. Old patterns tend to be reinforced unless a new discipline is introduced. Most of us will always take the path of least resistance.
3. There must be a system in place to monitor the **process** and **progress**.
4. Exposure to new experiences and skills designed to bring about change.
5. There should be evidence of self-sustaining motivation; in other words evaluate the degree to which you have to drive the process, and the degree to which the subject is motivated.
6. Is there a personal recognition or acknowledgement of the problem? Does the individual take responsibility for their behavior?
7. Allow for the presence of support. The change process requires the support of family, close friends, mentors, etc., outside of the "change agents". If there is no presence of support, substantial, long-term change is harder to realize.
8. Skilled help must also be included in the change process. There must be an expertise introduced to insure that change occurs properly and in a healthy manner. What new wisdom is being added?

9. Finally, we should be able to "see" movement. Is progress being made? Change doesn't happen overnight, but we have a reasonable expectation to hope when we see progress being made."

"It is always better to jump than to wait to be pushed." Learn how to **end well**.

- **Protecting the Anointing on Your Life and Ministry**

In life, business and ministry – all we have are our relationships. The adversary's sole purpose in life is to steal, kill and destroy those relationships through disunity, division, discord, and deception. I believe we preserve the blessing and anointing of God on our lives when we walk in the light as He is in the light. When we walk in darkness, we break fellowship with God and each other. Light and darkness cannot co-exist together. Light exposes the deeds of darkness, and that exposure will cause conflict and opposition.

God gave me a word – a command to "speak truth to power" in that situation with the leadership. He said they would not listen because they were rebellious, but to say it anyway. (Ezekiel 2:5-8) At first, I talked myself out it because I reasoned that they would not listen, they did not care, and that it would make no difference at all. However, I became increasingly disturbed by the fact that I did not deliver the Word of the Lord.

One day I consulted another woman of God whom I respected and was seasoned in these matters. I wanted to know if it was too late. She recounted the story of Jonah and how God sent him to deliver a message to the people of Ninevah. Jonah tried with great effort to avoid his assignment, but eventually, after many dangers, toils and snares, he surrendered in obedience! She pointed out that there is no way to know how much time had elapsed while Jonah was running. It may have been several days – even months – before he turned around and went to Ninevah. The point is: It was not too late.

Like Jonah, I stopped running and I promptly delivered the message God gave me to speak to them. What a relief! The lesson here: ***it's never too late to walk in obedience. Obedience protects the anointing on our lives and ministry.*** Leave the results to God.

I don't take myself too seriously; that's just not who I am. However, I do take the call of God on my life very seriously. As much as it lies within me, I will not treat the call and ministry entrusted to me carelessly and without regard. It grieves the Spirit of God. Therefore, I am committed to be careful not to allow myself to be compromised by the sins of another for personal gain or selfish ambition.

Inasmuch as we are called as Ambassadors of Christ to prepare the way of the Lord in this end-time hour, it is important that we uphold Kingdom living and expose the deeds of darkness. It is our responsibility to preserve God's house and the ministry of the Gospel. I know it's hard for all kinds of reasons, but we will give an account to a much higher authority.

If at any time you recognize the following responses on the part of leadership, it is time for you to respond:

- failure to adhere to Church policy;
- failure to follow professional recommendations for proper documentation of actions to address the issue;
- failure to submit and adhere to the requests of management on matters of significance;

Sometimes you will observe that there is a hidden agenda. Others leaders may exhibit no desire to take responsibility and walk in their God-given authority. Unrepentance, lack of submission to or accountability to senior leadership, an unwillingness to seek and submit to professional assistance: all of these responses are an indication that something is wrong and that a response is necessary.

At first, this seems really scary because we have invested a lot of our time, talent and treasure into every ministry of which we are a part. We have developed relationships and established a life of ministry, but what we don't want is "our good to be evil spoken of." Therefore, let's protect the anointing on our lives and ministry. Let's declare together that we will not knowingly support or contribute to deceptive and ungodly behavior from those in spiritual authority.

The Anointing of Order

"When the queen of Sheba heard about the fame of Solomon and his relationship to the LORD, she came to test Solomon with hard questions. Arriving at Jerusalem with a very great caravan—with camels carrying spices, large quantities of gold, and precious stones—she came to Solomon and talked with him about all that she had on her mind. Solomon answered all her questions; nothing was too hard for the king to explain to her. When the queen of Sheba saw all the wisdom of Solomon and the palace he had built, the food on his table, the seating of his officials, the attending servants in their robes, his cupbearers, and the burnt offerings he made at the temple of the LORD, she was overwhelmed. She said to the king, "The report I heard in my

own country about your achievements and your wisdom is true. But I did not believe these things until I came and saw with my own eyes. Indeed, not even half was told me; in wisdom and wealth you have far exceeded the report I heard. How happy your people must be! How happy your officials, who continually stand before you and hear your wisdom! Praise be to the LORD your God, who has delighted in you and placed you on the throne of Israel. Because of the LORD's eternal love for Israel, he has made you king to maintain justice and righteousness."
And she gave the king 120 talents[b] of gold, large quantities of spices, and precious stones. Never again were so many spices brought in as those the queen of Sheba gave to King Solomon."
(1Kings 10:1-10)

THE ANOINTING OF ORDER

Where there is confusion, there is envy, selfish ambition, and every evil work. (James 3:16) Without **order** there is confusion, discord, discontent, distrust, high turnover, low morale, stunted growth and burdensome service.

As a certified human resources professional and trainer, with more than 15 years of experience as a Human Resources Officer in full-time ministry, my passion is to see ministry and service delivered with joy and excellence; to transform ministry staff culture in a way that restores vision and engagement and re-ignites passion for ministry.

Did you know there is a direct relationship between the "anointing" and "order"? Well, there is, and I want to share with you some insights on the importance of structure in ministry affairs from a Biblical perspective.

There are biblical principles that emphasize the importance of establishing order in the administration of Church affairs, and when applied in combination with professional guidance and coaching, will assist faith-based and non-profit organizations in generating new life, vision and passion in their staff and leadership.

Let's look at 1 Kings 10:1-10

Principle # 1 *Let all things be done in decency and in order* (1 Cor. 14:40). God is not the author of confusion. (1 Cor. 14:33).

As human beings we may not always recognize it or want to admit it, but we need structure, discipline in order to live productive and effective lives. Have you ever pondered why? Let me share a few reasons:

- To make wise decisions
- To be good stewards
- To attract and develop the best leaders and staff
- To be more effective in ministry to the Body of Christ
- To develop new leaders
- To be a witness in the community
- To strategically and effectively prepare for change and growth

- To fulfill and sustain the mission and vision of the Church
- To establish and maintain a healthy environment for leaders and ministry to flourish

God has used me to bring order and structure to organizations with more than 100 employees, where there were no HR policies and procedures in place, and no records of time and attendance. Employees were constantly coming to me asking how much vacation or sick time they had. Some thought a record was being kept somewhere, and others, who were a little more diligent, kept their own records. I had to pretty much take them at their word. But it wasn't their fault! This was the way they were used to operating: on "the honors" system! My task was to establish an HR Department that served both the leadership and the staff. However, their system of operation up to that point was very costly to the organization–as we will see a little later.

Principle #2 *An unjust weight is an abomination in the sight of God.* (Proverbs 20:23)

The organization in our first example also had no current, written job descriptions for any of the employees. Therefore, there were some employees whose workload

The Anointing of Order

far outweighed that of others in the same category. This resulted in an undue burden which employees shouldered for many years. Many of them had not had raises in five or more years, while the leadership enjoyed regular increases. Several resigned for just that reason. Thus, employee morale was at an all-time low. This ought not be in the Body of Christ.

There are always employees who appear to be willing to go above and beyond, but beneath the façade, they were actually seething with resentment because they did not feel at all valued or rewarded for their sacrifice of service. This undercurrent of resent manifested itself in several ways: lack of participation and support of church events and special services, little or no input or creativity for special projects, little or no financial commitment, and very low employee engagement in the overall mission and goals of the organization.

One organization hired an outside professional consulting company to conduct an employee and membership survey. When it was completed, the results were rather disturbing. Not only was the staff extremely disgruntled, but the membership had some pretty strong things to say as well. To add insult to injury, the senior leader was so outraged by the results, that he completely disregarded the whole project, fired the staff leader whom he appointed to

The Way Makers

spearhead the project, and then proceeded to conduct his own survey! Needless to say everyone was even more outraged! Many felt their concerns were disregarded and dishonored. They felt even more demoralized and devalued. Slowly, but surely, staff and membership began to dwindle as those who suffered in silence took their leave.

Service should always be life giving and life sustaining – not a burden and a chore – no matter what type of organization in which it is rendered.

In our text, each member of the palace is happy, smiling, and *performing his/her assigned responsibilities*. No square pegs in round holes here! In the following verses, we see a stark contrast in the attitude and disposition of Solomon's staff. (1 Kings 4:1-19; 1 Kings 10:8) **Order is visible and spiritual. This brings me to my final point:**

Principle #3 *Render unto Caesar that which is Caesar's; obey the laws of the Land* (acting in accordance with what has been set in place by governmental authority). (1 Kings 10:1-2)

This is not just referring to taxes, but godly stewardship of our time, our resources (especially human resources), and our commitment to the mission and vision of the organization, within the context of

The Anointing of Order

employment or service. That includes compliance with the laws governing employment, fair/minimum wages, healthcare, discrimination and immigration.

We are on dangerous ground when we begin to subscribe to the theory that "you are to work as unto the Lord" to justify our mistreatment of others. The scriptures are very clear that we are to be good to all who serve, but ***especially*** those of the household of faith (Gal. 6:10). We are not to prefer Pastors/leaders only, but ALL who serve in full-time ministry. Employees are to be paid a fair wage, commensurate with their duties and responsibilities. If the world can take care of its own, how much more should we take care of The Body of Christ? It is the charge of leadership to cultivate such an environment of care and trust. Let's look at some examples of and the potential consequences of disorder in an organization:

Organization A was in trouble with the bank. They had not had a full-scale, certified audit in years. Why? They didn't want to pay for it. On the heels of that, they discover bookkeeping inconsistencies revealing embezzlement; there were IRS fines and the accounting records were in serious disarray. To fix all of the issues – with professional fees and employee man hours – would cost them almost half a million dollars. Major action had to be taken to prevent foreclosure from the bank, which they had every right to do. Needless to say, they barely made it through without a major collapse of the entire organization.

Organization B had a large number of staff working with children and youth who had not had background checks done in years. Why? They did not want to pay for them. Several of the senior leaders, with governmental authority, had no confidentiality or non-disclosure agreements.

Also, there were employees on staff who were out of status with immigration, and most employees with tenure of eight years or more, had to be recertified. If they had an audit at that point in time, they would have received a hefty fine and could have forfeited their tax-exempt status. That is serious!

God equipped and used me to establish order, structure and compliance. Please let me be clear: This is not an indictment against anyone, but simply to impress upon all of us the importance of order and structure with respect to human resources management and leadership development in an organization.

Notwithstanding all of that, below is a personal testimony of how painful non-compliance can be and the impact it has on the Body of Christ...

Susan had been working for the organization for well over 10 years. She and her husband were practically permanent fixtures

The Anointing of Order

there. They raised their daughter there and everyone was enormously fond of them. They served faithfully in the ministry. Susan and her husband soon became good friends of me and my husband. In fact, her husband, Sam, was especially gracious toward me when my aunt died, and my husband had been out of work for several months. Resources were very limited at the time I was to go to North Carolina for her funeral. Sam took me the train station, walked me to the train, and on my return, he not only came to pick me up, but he came inside and looked for me to guide me out of the station. (I don't travel on public transportation that much, and being in the huge maze of Union Station was quite intimidating to me.) So Sam's attentiveness and care was a special blessing to me. It eased and comforted me during a time that was otherwise, emotionally and physically draining.

All during the ride home, Sam encouraged me with one word after another. When we arrived at my house–that we were in danger of losing due to my husband's unemployment–Sam stayed with me and prayed over my marriage, my husband's employment and the safe keeping of our home. It was very special and our friendship was sealed that day. When I began to serve in public ministry, Sam and his wife were the first to come and share their testimony with my congregation! We had history. But I had no idea how disorder in the organization would later threaten our friendship.

The time would come when Sam would be diagnosed with advanced stage cancer. For the first year and a half, we were very encouraged and looked forward to long-term remission. Susan was still working for the organization, but she only worked part time, and was now the only source of income for their household. Just when Sam suffered a serious setback, requiring more surgery and chemotherapy, I was doing an I-9 audit. What I discovered would dramatically change the course of our friendship.

I called Susan to my office to notify her that her immigration documents on file had expired and she needed to provide updated documents. Sam was in the hospital, and everyone was praying because the situation was very touch-and-go. I extended grace and gave more grace in consideration of all that they were going through, but the time came when I had to put the pressure on her to produce the required documents. I hated to do this because these were my friends and I loved them. We served in ministry together and they were the first to support my public ministry. The whole situation was emotionally charged, and yet I had a job to do. The thing I feared the most came upon me: I had to meet with Susan to notify her of her release from employment due to I-9 non-compliance. She was extremely angry and said some

The Anointing of Order

extremely hurtful things. A meeting with her and Sam, and senior management followed.

Professionally, it was also one of the hardest things I ever had to do. Emotionally, it was extremely draining: my emotions ran the gamut from compassion, to sorrow, to anger, to loneliness, to just wanting to run and hide. I wanted to be anywhere but there.

Many weeks passed without a word from my friends. We would see each other in Church, but never a word transpired. During this time, I came under attack: I was judged and misunderstood by others in the Body of Christ – mostly, because they were misinformed. I saw Susan several times at the office and one day, God gave me an opportunity to express my sorrow at hearing the news of Sam's setback. He did eventually make it back to Church and one Sunday, we (my husband and I) saw Sam and he greeted us! We spoke kindly to one another and I knew all had been forgiven. I believe this was the Lord's doing – to allow us the opportunity to be reconciled to each other.

Sam eventually lost his battle with cancer and my heart was broken in a million pieces. I attended the service, of course, but his home-going was bittersweet. I am forever grateful to God that we were able to forgive and be forgiven before Sam went home to be with The Lord. This was a sad and tragic end to an emotionally and spiritually volatile situation. Through God's grace, we overcame.

Relationally, as for me, God is my vindication. Many would be surprised to know the opposition and accusation I suffered in that situation. But I stood on God's Word, "No weapon formed against me shall prosper. Every tongue that rose up against me shall be shown to be in the wrong." (Isa. 54) Leadership often comes with a very high price.

Professionally, I know I did the right thing for the right reasons. These were serious infractions that the government takes an exceptionally dim view. The consequences for the organization could have been catastrophic if there was any kind of government investigation, e.g., fines, a cease and desist order, revocation of tax-exempt status and even imprisonment.

Lack of order in the house of God is just poor stewardship. Consistent practice of poor stewardship (of human or financial resources) leads to consistent disobedience. There are consequences for disobedience. (Luke 16) When we misuse unrighteous mammon and mistreat God's people, who can trust us with the "true riches"? It is evident from our text that "true riches" refers to matters of the Kingdom: The Anointing, Unity of the Body, and Salvation.

The Anointing of Order

The Anointing of Order is manifested in Solomon's palace (1 Kings 4:1-19; 1 Kings 10:8):

- Attitude and Disposition of Staff – They were smiling and obviously happy to serve!
- Each member performing his/her assigned responsibilities
- Succession Planning–Continuity – Leadership Transition – They did their jobs well. Paul said, "the things you've heard me say and seen me do, the same commit to faithful men." You are required from this example, to train, to equip prospective leaders, and commit your knowledge, experience and mentorship to faithful men.
- Order instills and perpetuates confidence and trust in the ministry (inside and outside)
- Financial prosperity resulted from the Queen's observation of the palace order.
- The Anointing of Order – Glorify and Honor God (2 Chron. 9:8; 9:12)

Without order there is confusion, stunted growth, discord, discontent, high turnover, low morale and burdensome service. Underutilization of human resources leads to malnourishment to the Body of

Christ. Without ***order*** there are eternal implications:

- Ineffective ministry in the Body of Christ
- Division
- Weakened Witness (internally and externally)
- Grieve the Holy Spirit and Forfeit the Anointing
- The Body of Christ is Malnourished
- Ineffective in our assignment and failure to fulfill The Great Commission

We will give an account for everything we've done in the body – whether good or evil. Jesus is coming back! And He's coming back for a Church without spot or wrinkle, and I believe our mandate is to not only "occupy until He comes" or "do business until He comes", but to do it *in decency and in order*. So, if Jesus were to return tomorrow, would He find your house in order?

Where there is confusion, there is envy, selfish ambition, and every evil work.

The Anointing of Order

Turning Passion into Purpose!

"So Christ himself gave the apostles, the prophets, the evangelists, the pastors and teachers, to equip his people for works of service, so that the body of Christ may be built up." (Eph. 4:11-12)

TURNING PASSION INTO PURPOSE!

God has spoken. It is a new season! It is my season to step into divine purpose! God has called me to raise up millions of Way Makers all over the world! He has anointed me to preach The Gospel (to bind up the broken-hearted, to set the captive free, to open the eyes of the blind and to preach the acceptable year of the Lord), to equip the saints for the work of the ministry, and to establish order in His House.

We spend so much time worrying about who is going to run for President in the next election, when and how we are going to retire, or when we are going to start that new business, etc., etc. (Matt. 16:3) But if you are a Way Maker, you are keenly aware of the time in which we are living, and you know what you should be doing. (Matt. 24; Eph. 5:15-17)

Equipping the Saints for the Work of the Ministry

As Way Makers, Ambassadors for Christ, our assignment is to prepare **the way** of the Lord. That means we are responsible for making sure that we are ready to receive the end-time harvest of souls into the Kingdom. The task at hand is to train, coach and raise up leaders who are equipped for the work of the ministry–namely, the evangelist, the teacher and the prophet. Jesus gave us the five-fold ministry gifts specifically for this purpose (Eph. 4:11-12). Evangelists sow and water the seed of The Word; God gives the increase. Teachers make disciples by giving instruction in the foundational truths of the faith. The prophetic ministry will play a critical role in declaring the proceeding word of God to the Body of Christ. It is so important that we have ears to hear what the Spirit of the Lord is *saying*. It is their responsibility to give divine instruction, direction and encouragement to Body of Christ concerning end-time affairs.

Most often, the role of the evangelist is overlooked in terms of seeking out and cultivating this gift in the Body; in contrast, the gift of teaching is more widely recognized, but often as a pastoral gifting. But God has designed this gift to be a separate and major support to the pastoral gift to build up and edify the Body of Christ. Pastors and leaders must begin to seek out, recognize and cultivate these ministry gifts in the Body of Christ. It is absolutely essential to end-time Kingdom work.

Thom Rainer and Chuck Lawless conducted a Healthy Church Survey[7] in which 160 questions were asked to assess the condition of the Church in the 6 key purposes of the Church (worship, evangelism, discipleship, ministry, prayer and fellowship). They reported on the most common responses to areas of weakness. Two such areas were reported as follows:

Discipleship and evangelism are the weakest areas in the church. *I cannot recall the last survey that showed other areas as the weakest. Again and again, these churches admit they struggle in doing evangelism and discipleship – two non-negotiable components of the Great Commission* (Matt. 28:16-20). (**Ref.** http://tinyurl.com/kvvd6d8)[7]

Members say they would do more evangelism if they had more training. *Whether or not they actually would do more is another matter, but we simply report what the church tells us. Members tell us that fears keep them from evangelizing, and they would welcome more training.* (**Ref.** http://tinyurl.com/kvvd6d8)[7]

God has Transformed My Passion into Purpose!

By the time you read this chapter, Angelic Grace Ministries International, Inc. will be born. Our mission is fully described in this book. The Gracey Group LLC[9] is the for-profit arm that specializes in leadership training and coaching for faith-based and non-profit organizations and emerging businesses. God has put a word in my mouth and a burden on my heart to not only equip, encourage and inspire, but to **protect** the Body of Christ. I have emerged a much stronger leader as a result of my experiences and lessons learned; I want to commit the same to faithful men and women of God – The Way Makers.

We are all passionate about something; some of us can identify our passions more easily than others. Our passion can be born out of tragedy or triumph. The thing is we don't always know what to do or HOW to do something meaningful about our passions. I want to share with you the story of my journey.

I started my career in corporate America at IBM for 10 years, which culminated in transition when I received revelation from God to go back to school. I did, and half way through my studies, God called me to work full-time in ministry as Executive Assistant to the Chief Executive Officer of our Church organization.

This was a dramatic change for me. I was very skeptical. I pulled my application back three times! Although I didn't realize it at the time, there was a lot of opposition. People, who were supposed to be my friends, were saying things to intimidate me from accepting my new position as HR Generalist and Assistant to the CEO. That decision changed my life from that point on. My life has never been the same. I served in that capacity for 6 years, during which time I experienced tremendous growth, marriage, and leadership development.

One rainy day in 1997, just one year after we were married, we were returning home from Church, when the bottom fell out. It would prove to be only the first of one of the most emotionally painful experiences in my life as a Christian. Moral failure on the part of senior leadership caused many to leave the Body of Christ – including many of our close friends. I was still serving on staff, so it was an especially painful time for me. I remember...it was during that time when I came to know the Lord as my refuge. I hid in Him – in the secret place of His pavilion, I escaped. It took a very long time for my husband and me to recover from the emotional trauma of that experience. But thanks be to God who makes us victorious through Christ Jesus!

Opportunity In the Midst of Chaos

Progress often comes by way of adversity. Adversity has a way of causing us to refocus and see things – our lives – from a new perspective. Such was the case for me. In was in the chaos of that situation that my eyes were opened to the possibility and the Kairos timing of God to pursue my dream of entrepreneurship. As I began to abide in the presence of God, my passion was ignited and the vision for Rhema Writing Concepts was birthed in my spirit in 1998. For the next six years, I served the small business and non-profit communities as a conference speaker, writer, trainer and consultant and eventually, authored **"Starting a Business on a Shoestring Budget"**, a how-to handbook for emerging entrepreneurs!

Passion Re-Ignited

I remained steadfast in faith and continued to abound in the work of the Lord. ***My passion was re-ignited:*** My book was selling well in Borders Books, Basic Black Books, and a few smaller book stores throughout the City of Philadelphia. I enjoyed doing book signings and the success and recognition from my peers and colleagues in business and in local government. It was the year 2000, and we had transitioned to another place of worship. Still, God began to open doors of opportunity in leadership. My husband and I loved small group ministry and had both served in leadership roles, so we were delighted when we were asked to train the leaders in our congregation to be able to implement Small Group Ministry in the Church. Of course, we were met with resistance and opposition, but we persevered and completed our assignment.

In 2001, God spoke to us prophetically and that word would lead us away from all things familiar. My business did well for the next few years. I was even able to secure a private office outside of my home. My husband was completing his undergraduate degree, so we were pretty sure we would not leave Philadelphia before then. But as the date for graduation drew closer and closer, things began to dry up in my business. After graduation in May 2003, I moved my office back home and waited for God's direction. We knew we would eventually leave so we avoided renewing the lease on our apartment and moved in with a friend temporarily. We mistakenly thought the vision for our move was afar off and began to look for a house. Needless to say, God closed that door, so we waited for more direction, until…

Death of the Vision–A Personal Crisis

During the summer of 2003, I had been experiencing a painful cramp in my left leg

The Way Makers

for weeks. I thought I had pulled a muscle because of all the strenuous activity of physically moving my office. I went on, nursing the pain with over-the-counter drugs, until it was time for our annual leadership conference. My husband and I both attended, and as soon as we got there, my leg began to swell to almost twice its normal size. It was extremely painful, and I still had no idea what was going on. Someone said they thought it was a blood clot. I didn't think so; that seemed so extreme! Besides, I thought to myself: How in the world could that happen? Well it did.

Immediately upon our return, Tony insisted that I go straight to the hospital. I was in so much pain I literally crawled across the parking lot and sat on the curb, while Tony went to get a wheelchair. Once the doctors determined it was a clot, they sprang into action: hooking me up to IV's, heart monitors and pumping me with pain killers and blood thinners – all in an effort to keep the clot from moving. I was surrounded by 7 or 8 doctors and nurses in the Emergency Room. Tears were streaming down my face and I was in so much pain I could hardly talk. As I lay there, trying to wrap my mind around the severity of my situation, I turned to God. I knew that if He didn't stop that blood clot in its tracks, I was going to die. I wanted to say something to comfort my husband, but I couldn't. I couldn't say good-bye because I wasn't ready to die! I wanted to fight! I wanted to believe God would save me! So I prayed. I cried and I prayed. That was December 18, 2013.

My husband stayed with me until late that night, but eventually he had to go home. I was alone and I prayed that I would live to see him the next day. The dawn made its debut with my eyes still open. I was afraid to go to sleep. The next few days were difficult to say the least. By this time, my left leg was locked in position, bent at the knee with my left foot touching my right knee. I could not walk and, unless it was of physical necessity, most movement was strictly prohibited until the clot dissolved. I needed a lot of help and I didn't know what to do. All I could think of was how was I going to get past this? Well, that blood clot would eventually lead to something even more horrifying!

It was December 23rd; I had been in the hospital for five days now. The doctors were concerned about my heart, so they wanted to do a stress test. I was still unable to walk, so they had to induce the test while I was lying down. Everything seemed to be going fine, until I heard a number of rapid beeps from the monitors. I felt kind of funny, but I thought it was just the technician doing the test. That was not the case. All of a sudden, one of the nurses said, "She's crashing! She's crashing! Stay with me Mrs. Gracey!" I'm thinking what is she talking about? I'm

The Way Makers

not crashing! Everything seemed to be in slow motion. My mind was fuzzy and I felt like I couldn't breathe even though I was breathing. I soon realized that my heart rate had dropped to a dangerously low level. I could have died right there on the table! I was mortified! I thought: The enemy is trying to kill me again! Somehow – it was God's grace and healing touch that pulled me back – I recovered. They gave me a shot of something and my heart rate stabilized.

Later that afternoon, a cardiologist came to my room, asking some really disturbing questions. One of them was, "Has anyone in your family ever died suddenly for no apparent reason?" I could tell he was much younger than me, so I chalked up his blatant insensitivity to the ignorance of youth! He proceeded to tell me what my diagnosis was and that if I did not have heart surgery for a pacemaker implant the very next morning – Christmas Eve!–I would not live to see the New Year! I was so shocked! I was confused, angry and highly agitated.

At first, I completely shut him down and refused to have the surgery. Shortly, thereafter, an elderly man, whom I always describe as "Colonel Sanders" because he looked just like him! Anyway, the Colonel proceeded to read me the riot act about refusing the surgery, emphatically informing me that I was obviously not aware of the gravity of my situation. I was so mad! But

Turning Passion Into Purpose!

I respectfully yielded to his command and humbly apologized to the cardiologist for being so rude. Usually when I feel like that, all I can do is cry. I called my husband, but I could barely get the words out of my mouth. I couldn't believe I had to let them cut my body! Everything in me wanted to rebel! But deep down, I knew I had no choice.

The next several hours were a blur. The nurses were trying to tell me to stop crying as it only raised my blood pressure, but I couldn't help it. All kinds of thoughts went through my head: What if I don't survive the surgery? I was on blood thinners; what if I bled to death on the table? I had no time to put my affairs in order! I wasn't finished! Oh God! How was I going to fulfill the call on my life? He called me to raise up Way Makers! How was I going to do that now? I couldn't even walk! What about my husband? My beloved Tony – he had experienced so much loss already! Now he's going to lose his wife too? Oh no, God! Please! I was still in the throes of this horror movie in my head, when several members of our Church, including the Assistant Pastor, showed up at my door to pray, but by that time, the vision had died.

Everyone looked so somber. That was not very comforting, but then I realized that this was a very serious situation. As they began to pray, I stopped crying. The Assistant Pastor began to sing a song prophetically.

He just sang to me for a while and I felt the peace of God come in and suddenly I wasn't afraid. They eventually left, but afterward, I lay quietly, listening to God. He began to tell me that this was not a sickness unto death. He said we were going to go through this together. "Just you and Me" He said. "We're going through this together." It was a momentary stop, that's all. He said, "We have to do this first, then we are going to move on." I clung to those words for the rest of the night.

As they began to prep me for surgery, I kept repeating those words over and over again in my head. The nurses and everyone were being super nice and supportive. They assured me that I had the best surgeon in the country – one of only a handful of experts on my condition – and that I was going to be fine. The nurse was holding my hand, and I was listening to my song. That was the last thing I remembered.

I came through the procedure with flying colors. Although I eventually made a full recovery, it was a long and painful process. It would take months of physical therapy before I could walk normally again. I finally left the hospital on New Year's Eve! I know God was with me during that entire ordeal. Later, although I was still using a walker to support my body, I was able to return to Church.

A Personal Encounter with God

My first Sunday back, our Pastor acknowledged and welcomed me back at the start of the service. Then, as was his custom, he began to minister prophetically in song. These were special times of worship that I reveled in! I loved the way the Spirit of God would move through him in prophetic worship. This was a very special time. He continued in worship and then he began to sing the very words God had spoken to me in the hospital! I erupted in tears of worship! God was confirming to me that it was Him who was speaking to me! He let me know that He heard me! He never left me and He carried me through! Nobody else knew! It was just between me and God. It was a beautiful melody…*"It's just Me and you, you and Me, we're going through…together."* I will never forget the most profound way God met me that day.

I thought my illness meant the death of my destiny, but that was not the case. The Lord has determined all of my days; not one of them will be cut short until He says so. However, dramatic change was coming that would again threaten my sense of direction and stability in God.

New Beginnings

The Word of the Lord Bishop Coleman prophesied three years earlier about our leaving Philadelphia, had come to pass. In the spring of 2004, my husband was offered a professional post with honors at the U.S. Department of Justice. We were moving to Washington, DC. In September of that year, we arrived in Silver Spring, MD–one day short of our eighth wedding anniversary (eight is the number for "new beginnings).

I had to close my business and relocate to whole new state! We had no family or friends in Maryland or DC. I personally did not want to move to this particular area because it was where the John Malvo sniper shootings took place and one of the planes on September 11, 2001, crashed into the Pentagon! This was not my first pick! But God was in control. Shortly after we arrived, I found myself going through a period of mourning – grieving the loss of all that was familiar (friends, family, Church, business, colleagues, network, etc.) It was also during this brief interlude in my life, that I enter "Sanctuary" as I referred to earlier in the book.

Passion Re-ignited for Service

This time, personal adversity opens the door for new opportunities! Fully recovered and armed with a whole new set of experiences and life lessons, and with a fresh start in a new place, I embarked on a 7-year assignment in full-time ministry as a Human Resources Officer. During my tenure, I was commissioned and ordained to the ministry; received my SHRM Professional Certification and IBTA Business Professional Certification; began public ministry; and became a published writer and conference speaker. As I discussed earlier, one of the most significant areas of growth for me was emotional healing through servant leadership and participation in Celebrate Recovery – a ministry of inner healing out of Saddleback Church, under the leadership of Pastor Rick Warren.

The Vision Resurrected

The other significant area of growth was maturity in the call of God on my life. I was pregnant with a vision and my belly was growing! I was in my second trimester. My capacity was enlarging and I began to nurture the seed in my womb! God sovereignly orchestrated a conference to be held at our Church, and I was invited to be the main speaker at our kick-off breakfast! The theme: "Prepare the Way of the Lord!" In 2005, the vision was resurrected and I began to declare the message God had given me. Soon, The Way Makers course and blog of the same name were born! **www.theway-makers.blogspot.com**

The Call to Transition

The contractions have started again! The second moral failure on part of leadership would rear its ugly head again and threaten to distract me and cause me to lose focus. But not this time! I'd rather obey God, than man. I cannot afford to waste time trying to please men. Once again, adversity would prepare the way for promotion. Whenever the norm is disturbed, it forces us to see with new eyes. It is at these times, we become aware of the growth and maturity that has taken place in our lives. In other words, we find out what we're made of! We find out that we are wiser, stronger and more equipped than ever before. We come to realize that although there were small beginnings, the vision was yet for an appointed time, and that time is now! I'm in the third trimester! It's time to PUSH! Ready or not, this baby is coming!

God spoke to me, "Write the book. Write the vision. Take My message to the people; then the fire will come." And so ***"The Way Makers–Ambassadors for Christ, Preparing the Way of the Lord"*** is born!

Turning My Passion into End-time Purpose

In this end-time hour, God has called me to equip, empower and inspire leaders to take their place as Way Makers and fulfill their Kingdom purpose in these last days. My passion is ignited with an increased burden for:

- Healing the professionally and spiritually abused
- Those discouraged and disillusioned in service
- Relieving the burden of the business side of ministry on leadership
- Reversing the drain of human and financial resources of organizations due to lack of boundaries, unhealthy spirituality and unaccountability
- The restoration of passion, vision, joy and morale – that are overshadowed by fear, complacency, suspicion and selfish ambition.

I know that there are many other faith-based and non-profit organizations who share the same challenges. I consider it a divine calling to come along side to support and strengthen as the Lord leads. God admonishes us that when we have come through, to turn again and strengthen the brethren. (Luke 22:32)

God admonishes us that when we have come through, to turn again and strengthen the brethren. (Luke 22:32)

To that end, I founded The Gracey Group LLC (www.thegraceygroupllc.com)[9] to see ministry and leadership administered with unity, joy and excellence, and to transform organizational culture by increasing morale, restoring vision and re-igniting passion!

So whether you are a Pastor, Minister or leader, leading a faith-based or non-profit organization, or wanting to establish a new organization, my sole mission is to help you **turn your passion into purpose!**

PREPARING THE WAY OF THE LORD

Jesus is coming back for His Bride – a Church without spot or wrinkle.

Will He find faithful, sober, vigilant men and women of God with their lamps full of oil? Will we be found with a righteousness of our own, or the righteousness that only comes through faith in Jesus Christ?

Will He find His House in order, or will He find the Church like Moses did when he came down off the mountain – drunken and disorderly?

The answer to those questions depends on us!

> Are you ready to enlist in God's end-time army?
>
> Are you prepared to assume office as an Ambassador of Christ?

If you answered yes, I want to hear from you! We have an assignment. We are launching The Way Makers Leadership Development Summit and we need leaders who are ready to enlist and serve!

Contact Us at: missmsgr@aol.com or www.angelicgraceministries.org

For **Organizational Support** visit: www.thegraceygroupllc.com

Submit contact info for updates and events.

Subscribe to our **Blog**: www.thewaymakers.blogspot.com

BIBLIOGRAPHY

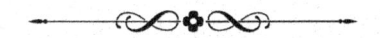

---

[1] **"Emotionally Healthy Spiritually"** by Peter Scazzaro, Thomas Nelson, 2006

[2] **"Still I Rise"** by Maya Angelou, New York, Random House, 1978

[3] **"Hearing God's Voice"** by Henry and Richard Blackaby, Broadman & Holman, 2002

[4] **"The Way of the Heart – Connecting with God through Prayer, Wisdom and Silence"** by Henri J. M. Nouwen,

[5] **"The Supernatural Power of the Transformed Mind"** by Bill Johnson, Destiny Image Publishers, Inc., 2005

[6] ***"Hearing God: 30 Different Ways"*** by Larry Kreider

[7] **"Healthy Church Survey"**, by Thom Rainer and Chuck Lawless, **Ref.** http://tinyurl.com/kvvd6d8

[8] **"Necessary Endings"** by Dr. Henry Cloud, Collins Publishers, 2010

[9] The Gracey Group LLC – www.TheGraceyGroupllc.com